Faith Walk:
Galatians for Women

By
Jennifer Maxey

Dedicated

in hope to

EL ELYON, the Most High God;

Jesus, KURIOS, my glorified Master and King;

HAGIOS PNEUMA, the Holy Breath, who seals and claims His people;

With special thanks to my husband, Kevin Maxey, who heard and re-heard every line, offering kindness, patience, and encouragement throughout the journey; to Mark Mayberry, who read and re-read every expression, with persevering dedication and diligence, often from "dawn til dusk" *literally*. Best editor ever.

ISBN-10: 1-58427-527-8

ISBN-13: 978-1-58427-527-5

Truth Publications, Inc.
CEI Bookstore
220 S. Marion St., Athens, AL 35611
855-492-6657
sales@truthpublications.com
www.truthbooks.com

Table of Contents

Lessons   **Page**

1. Why Galatians?   5

2. A Sower in Galatia   21

3. Spirit-Seed in Galatia   35

4. Flesh-Seed in Galatia   49

5. Soil in Galatia   73

6. Fruit in Galatia   87

Sources   109

Why Galatians?

Lesson 1: Introduction

Three weeks ago, I told a lie. It was one of those kinds of lies you do not plan to tell. Unplanned. It was one of those lies that just falls out of your mouth. Accidental. It was one of those lies that reveals what is really in your heart. Authentic. There it was. I lied.

Following my successful search for a stylishly collegiate bathroom towel shelf for my daughter, a helpful store assistant loaded it into my trunk. As she finished, he approached. Perhaps by design, he caught me off-guard. Immediately, that gaunt, disheveled appearance betrayed his lowly position in society: beggar; probable druggie. My instinctive reaction flashed: "Beware. Get away!"

Inwardly impatient, I interrupted his rehearsed plea for fast cash. "No need for explanations, Sir, I will give you some money. Here," I offered, pulling some cash out of my pocket, "You can have this." Then, during my good deed, I lied: "This is all the cash I have on me today. I hope it helps." Just like that, I lied. For no real reason, I lied. After decades of telling the truth, somehow, I lied.

Seven dollars. That's how much I handed over from the cash in my pocket.

Eighteen dollars and eleven cents. That's how much money I carried that day, leftover change from a twenty-dollar bill.

My External Deeds	My Internal Heart
"Righteous" deed	Irritation at his approach
Notice the beggar	See the beggar; do not see the man
Give money to the beggar	Give from excess; feel stingy even with excess
Give time to the beggar	Uncomfortable; just wanted him to leave
Smile at the beggar	Beggar to me; not a human; not a soul; relieved he is gone

How do you feel when you tell a lie? No woman of faith intends to tell lies. No woman of faith aspires to deceive. No woman of faith with $18 in her pocket purposefully proposes that it is only $7. Yet, sometimes it happens. So, how does that make you feel? For me, that day, the realization that I had lied—*sinned*—powerfully, and almost immediately, punched. My heart rate increased; my face flushed and burned; my stomach turned and soured. Alone in my car, I interrogated myself aloud, "Why did you do that?!"

For women walking by faith, the external fruit of our daily interactions reveals the internal condition of our hearts before God. Sacred Scripture reminds us, "For out of the abundance of the heart the mouth speaks" *(Luke 6:45)*, and "Every way of a man is right in his own eyes, but the Lord weighs the hearts" *(Prov. 21:2)*. Even deeper than that, these external manifestations of fruit disclose the internal heart seeds from which they originate. Over the last month, six months, one year, five years, ten years, which seeds have been sown, nourished, and developed within your heart? The fruit of some of those seeds may surprise you. Sometimes we mindlessly sow, nourish, or ignore heart seeds. Yet, God's word warns, "Do not be deceived; God is not mocked. Whatever a man sows that he will also reap" *(Gal. 6:7)*. External fruit reveals its source-seed.

Why Galatians?

This keystone concept of fruit disclosing the nature of its parent seed underpins the entire gospel story, finding particular emphasis in Galatians. Surprisingly, this study of Galatians started in the book of Matthew. I kept thinking about that day, so many years ago, when Jesus the Messiah, Immanuel *(i.e., "God-with-us")*, "went out of the house and sat beside the sea" *(Matt. 13:1)*. Understandably, considerable crowds surrounded Him, filled with anticipation. Mindfully, enthralled admirers stood on that beach, attending. "What will He say today?"

Behold, a sower went out to sow. As he sowed, some fell by the wayside, and the birds came and devoured them. Some fell upon rocky ground, where they had not much earth, and immediately they sprang up, because they had no depth of soil; and when the sun rose, they were scorched; and since they had no root, they withered away. Some fell among thorns, and the thorns grew up, and choked them. But other fell upon good ground, and produced fruit, some a hundredfold, some sixty, and some thirty. He who has ears to hear, let him hear (Matt. 13:2-3).

What would it have been like to be among the women of faith present that day? Could we have understood what Jesus wanted us to know, as He powerfully unveiled this foundational facet of the work of God among humanity?

Like most women of faith, I have been familiar with this parable about the sower. As I prayerfully studied through Paul's letter to Galatia, Immanuel's lesson emerged as a way to understand. In Galatians, several key concepts open our understanding of the scope and reality of God's intention for His seed in humanity. Throughout the book, all three unsuccessful soils become apparent. Further, as one of the earliest books of the New Testament, Galatians provides an on-the-ground, up-close examination of these parable principles at work.

In Jesus's allegory about the sower, everything seems so straightforward: *(1)* There are three kinds of unsuccessful soil: wayside, rocky, thorny; *(2)* There is one kind of productive soil: good; *(3)* There are three unsuccessful ends: birds eat the seed; shallow, rocky ground prevents root development resulting in withered, scorched plants; thorns take over and choke the growth of the

good seed; *(4)* There is one successful end: fruitfulness, some a hundredfold, some sixty, some thirty.

Just like us, every woman of faith in Galatia desired to be that good soil, bringing forth 100x fruit for the Master. And, like us, most of them also assumed that their hearts were, in fact, good soil. The wayside, rocky, and thorny soils must be about other people. Bad people. Surely not me, right? Surely not you. Furthermore, women of faith in Galatia aligned their wills for successful fruit-bearing. Feeling determined, some may have even made a checklist with a note to self:

How to Be Fruitful:
Love
Joy
Peace
Patience
Kindness
Goodness
Faithfulness
Gentleness
Self-control

There you go. I have chosen to follow this formula for fruitfulness. My heart must be good soil. I definitely want to bring forth fruit. So, I will do these fruits of the Spirit, and that will make me the hundredfold fruitful soil that Jesus talked about on the boat that day!

Except, it does not work that way. Spiritual fruit is not a "To-Do" list. Fruit is not forced. Fruit is not manifested overnight.

"Behold, a sower went forth to sow." Immanuel opened His mouth and taught the multitudes the parable of the sower, explaining God's sowing and reaping among and within human hearts. This life-promoting parable provides a framework for understanding the book of Galatians as more than a statement of historical facts about local congregations in Gaul. "He who has ears to hear, let him hear."

Why Not Galatians?

Galatians is tricky. As a woman of faith, my *(admittedly limited)* Galatian meditations before this study consisted primarily of two lists:

Works of the Flesh vs. Fruit of the Spirit

We should not view these concepts in isolation, separate from the rest of Paul's letter. Often, though, I have done precisely that. Here are some reasons I have not previously chosen a more comprehensive or contextual approach in studying Galatians:

- I didn't understand why Paul spent so much of the letter talking about himself.
- I didn't understand what Paul meant about Hagar and Sarah.
- I didn't understand what Paul meant about Law and Freedom.
- I didn't understand the details about how the Holy Spirit works in a Christian's life.
- I didn't understand how circumcision matters at all to women of faith.

Can you relate to these feelings about Galatians? If so, I encourage you to press a little deeper into the rich, challenging beauty of this Spirit-revealed text. Just because we may not understand everything in Paul's letter does not mean that we cannot understand anything. Through His word, our glorious God—Creator, Sustainer, Sovereign, True One—speaks to us. All the treasures of His carefully selected expression communicate the purpose, meaning, and understanding of the life of every woman of faith. Our eternal God calls us *(2 Tim. 1:9)* into a sacred, intimate relationship. Don't you want to know Him? Don't you want to know Him more? Let's grow in this grace and knowledge together.

Concepts in Galatia

Flesh to Spirit. Two opponents wage this war within each of us: Flesh and Spirit. Perhaps more than any other book, Galatians provides a clear delineation of these opposing sides. Some held tightly to certain aspects of their pre-conversion identity *(in this case, covenant circumcision as piety)*.

Identity by Flesh—Identity in Christ. Many of the converts in Galatia were confused and troubled by this distinction, not understanding that "in Christ neither circumcision nor uncircumcision avails anything, but a new creation" *(Gal. 6:15)*.

The works of the flesh reveal the ambitions of flesh: What I want, when I want it, how I want it, no matter who else is affected or destroyed. Why? Because flesh demands. Flesh takes. Flesh destroys. Flesh enthrones sin and self as master. When it is sown in the heart soil of one who chooses sin as master, the tender growth from God's pure seed withers in the waysides, rocks, and thorns.

In contrast, the fruit of the Spirit discloses the objectives of Spirit: What God wants, when He wants it, how He wants it, no matter who or what opposes or destroys me. Why should this matter? Because His way imparts life. Reaching forward to eternity, it saves. When sown in the heart soil of one who chooses God as Master, this pure seed thrives in the good soil that Jesus described. These two opponents, Flesh and Spirit, face off on the battleground of human hearts and minds. Which one is winning in you?

Slavery to Free-Will. God is sovereign, unmatched omnipotence—He must be obeyed. God is holy, untainted purity—He must be revered. God is just, unbiased impartiality—He must be feared. However, God reaches out to claim His own, not only from His exalted position and power but also from His enveloping love and light.

Our gracious God allows every individual the freedom to walk according to the flesh or the Spirit. By this choice, our actions externally manifest to God the inner nature of our heart soil. Although God has every right to demand and enforce obedience, He operates under a different mindset. He does not want us to choose His seed, the word, just because the law says so, or just because we are forced to do so. Instead, our Lord graciously offers us the choice to submit to the transforming, *dunamis* power of His living word *(Rom. 1:16; Heb. 4:12)*. He tenderly invites us to choose Him, voluntarily renouncing the world and its cares. There is no forced service here. Our sovereign, holy, and just God desires free-will obedience.

Free-will service can be challenging to understand, but God exhibits Abraham as an example of one who made the right choice. Abraham's choices revealed to God the good soil of his heart. Abraham chose the

Almighty God—before the covenant of circumcision and before the Law of Moses *(Gen. 12:1-9)*. Abraham lived before Moses's law. He chose God before the law. He trusted and obeyed God before the law. This is freedom, not forced service.

Law Is Slavery. By returning to the Law of Moses, rather than emulating the free-will faith of Abraham, the troublers in Galatia exhibited a slavery mindset.

In the countryside, a group of fifty men, women, and children labor rigorously in tattered clothes, digging a massive trench. Because they fail to look up, they never develop a relationship with the master. Never looking forward, they fail to discern the end purpose of their work—only that it is necessary to keep the directives. They endure a painstaking existence of blindly laboring, rarely succeeding. They are prisoners. The mindset of law is slavery.

Beginning with Ishmael, borne by the slave-woman Hagar, Abraham's seed by flesh were "slaves." "Now Hagar stands for Mount Sinai in Arabia and corresponds to the present city of Jerusalem because she is in slavery with her children" *(Gal. 4:25)*. Hagar is the covenant from Mount Sinai in Arabia *(4:23-24)*, which represents the law given to Moses. Hagar *(the Law of Moses)* bears children for slavery. This is Ishmael. This is flesh. This is law.

Paul equated returning to such a system as a yoke of slavery *(Gal. 5:1)*. Further, he said the binding of even one portion of that law represented a rejection of Christ's gracious gift. Beginning with, "If you accept circumcision" *(5:2)*, which equates to pre-conversion identity, Paul advises:

Christ will be of no advantage to you (5:2). You are then obligated to keep the whole law (5:3; cf. Jas. 2:1). You are severed from Christ if you seek to be justified by keeping law rules (5:4). You are fallen from grace if you seek to be justified by keeping law rules (5:4). You are hindered from obeying the truth (5:7), and this persuasion is not from Him who calls you (5:8).

In Galatia, circumcision as "required by God for salvation in Christ" threatened the message of Christ. Why did binding one part of the old system matter? Christ completed the law. He ended it, "having nailed it to the cross" (Col. 2:14). He met its demands, canceled our debt, and redeemed us. Returning to that system equates to a declaration of "Thanks, Jesus, but no thanks. We have the law."

Faith Is Freedom. Abraham's obedient faith emerged from a freedom mindset. The Law of Christ (Gal. 6:2), also called the Law of Liberty (Jas. 1:25), exemplifies this view.

In the countryside, a group of fifty men, women, and children labor rigorously in tattered clothes, digging a massive trench. Their master strives alongside, strengthening and encouraging. Throughout long, difficult days, he provides needed rest, nourishment, and water. Each morning, they gather to listen as their master reminds them of their vision and purpose. Each evening, they share excitement over progress and thanksgiving for such a thoughtful leader. They enjoy a life of freedom as volunteers laboring together to bring living water to forsaken villages. They are disciples. The mindset of faith is freedom.

Beginning with Isaac, the promised child of his wife Sarah, Abraham's seed by faith were free. Isaac, son of Abraham, entered the world according to faith (Heb. 11:11), born of the dead womb of an aged woman. Sarah is the covenant from Mt. Zion, the Jerusalem above, which is free (Gal. 4:26). Because Isaac was the child of promise, he was also born according to the Spirit (4:29), by faith (3:6). This is Isaac.

So, Isaac has other brothers and sisters like him, who are children of promise, because of faith. These brothers and sisters are Christians (Gal. 4:28). Christians, like Isaac, are born of Spirit (4:29; cf. John 3:5-8). Christians (like you and me), are brothers and sisters of Isaac! We are children of the promise, "not children of the slave, but of the free woman" (4:31). This is spirit. This is freedom.

"Obedient, but Free"

Taking away the curse and condemnation of the law, Jesus instituted a new way, which is the old way of Abraham: salvation by trusting, obedient faith. Now that Jesus filled up the legislated requirements of righteousness for the Mosaic code of law, it is completed. It has been satisfied. Nothing about God's righteous requirements in the law has been left undone. Now that it is completed, God calls us—Jew or Gentile, rich or poor, male or female—back to that free choice like Abraham displayed. Not because we have to. Not because God forces us. God desires obedience from freedom.

Conclusion

A closer look through the parable lens supplied by our Master Teacher opens our eyes to the spiritual battle scene, not only in Galatia but also in us. Yes, God the Sower and Jesus the Seed are at work, transforming our hearts and lives. Yet, they do not work unimpeded. An enemy follows close behind, dedicated to the destruction of their work in humanity *(and in us)*. Because of the enemy's work, our hearts often contain and nurture unrighteous seeds that must be discovered and uprooted.

It is like the lie I told. Unplanned. Accidental. Yet tragically authentic. I thank God for lessons learned that day. It opened my eyes to see the man, not the beggar. It led my steps back across the parking lot to find the soul, not the druggie. It opened my lips to encourage, not to scorn: "Sir, I heard you say that you believe in Jesus. I came back to tell you: *Jesus believes in you, too.*"

He started crying then and poured out his story of pain and abuse, drugs and gangs, prison and freedom, and the discovery that he has an eight-year-old son. He wants to do better for his son. He now begs, instead of depending on his former gang for support. He is getting up. He believes a better life is possible. And it is.

My prayer is that the seed of God will flourish in that man so that one day God's power will enable him to externally manifest that tiny, beautiful seed of faith that is in his heart now. All the way home with the decorative towel shelf, I also cried: For him, and his sin. For me, and my lie. For Jesus and His innocence. For God and His providence. Three weeks ago, I told a lie because the enemy's seeds of scorn and impatience grew for some time, undetected in my heart. Thankfully, the seed of God grew stronger within me, resulting in repentance and returning. As we enter this study of God's word in Galatia, how is your heart? Which seeds flourish in you?

Thought Questions

1. On a scale of 1 to 10, please rate your familiarity with Paul's letter to the Galatians?

2. Before embarking on this journey into Paul's letter, take a few moments for background research.

   Who were the Galatians?

How were Jews and Gentiles interacting in the region of Galatia?

3. Define the following:

Gentile

Gospel

Seed

Sower

Soil

Flesh

Spirit

Liberty

Freedom

Judgment

Mercy

4. What transforms a seed into fruit?

5. What is the relationship between flesh and spirit?

6. What is the difference between "keeping the law" and "free-will obedience?

7. God chose Abraham *(Gen. 12:1-9)*. **Why?** *(Gen. 18:19)*. **How can we know whether Abraham also chose God?**

8. At what point in history did Abraham believe God enough to obey Him?

9. What benefit will you receive by considering the gospel field of Galatia?

10. Which themes or passages in Galatians challenge you?

Concept Seeds

To begin preparation for the next lesson, please consider the following question:

What biblical principles should govern the way women of faith sow God's seed?

A Sower in Galatia

Lesson 2: Introduction

Has spring fever ever motivated you to plant a garden? If so, how did that work out for you? Did you have gardening success? For twenty-one years, spring fever has repeatedly, relentlessly driven me out to the soil with my container full of seeds. "Twenty-one years" sounds like a long time and a lot of gardening. "Twenty-one years" suggests the development of some expertise. Unfortunately, for me, "twenty-one years" flatly equates to twenty-one attempts and two and one-half successes. Naturally, this ratio introduces seeds of doubt into my gardening optimism.

Thankfully, sowing is not the same as gardening. Gardening is an extensive process, with various roles, duties, and deadlines, but sowing is simple. Get the seed to the soil. Every single year, I get the seed to the soil. This is something I can do! For twenty-one years, the seed-to-soil success ratio was 21:21. Yet, sowing is not the same as gardening.

Sowing 101

Introduce Seed to Soil
Introduce Seed to Soil
Introduce Seed to Soil
Introduce Seed to Soil

God desired fruit from Galatia. Namely, God desired the Spirit's fruit (*Gal. 5:22-23*). All fruit emerges from the seed, and seed distribution requires a sower. One day, the apostle Paul found himself in Galatia. His arrival there resulted from "bodily ailment" *(4:13)* of such severity that his condition severely strained the Galatians who cared for him. Even so, Paul declares, "I preached the gospel to you at first" *(4:13)*. The seed sown in Galatia was Jesus Christ, "who gave Himself for our sins to deliver us from the present evil age" *(1:4; 3:16)*. In Galatia, Paul sowed the gospel seed, the word of God *(1 Pet. 1:23)*, in the hope of fruit for God.

Paul was not always a sower. He became a sower. One day, on the road to Damascus, Jesus halted Saul of Tarsus with blinding light and a haunting question: "Saul, Saul, why are you persecuting Me?" *(Acts 9:4)*. The implications of the seed of Christ challenged Saul's core identity: his fundamental family loyalties, his ingrained devotion to the identifying traditions of his people; his entire life's trajectory.

The truth and authenticity of Jesus as God in the flesh practically nullified every pursuit of Paul's life until that moment *(Phil. 3:1-9)*. Despite the challenges of Saul's flesh identity, Jesus desired to develop within him. That day, Jesus halted Saul.

The seed, the word of God *(1 Pet. 1:23)*, took root and flourished in Paul's good-soil heart. Then, the seed brought forth another of its kind *(Gen. 1:11-12)*. What kind? The Christ-like kind. God "was pleased to reveal His Son" in him *(Gal. 1:16)*. Why? To transform Saul, the persecutor, into Paul, the apostle. Saul, the very Jewish Jew, was transformed into Paul, a preacher among Gentiles. The seed changed him from being flesh-focused to living a Spirit-focused life.

Paul developed into "fruit whose seed is in itself" *(Gen. 1:11)*. As good ground receives the seed, Paul heard the Word and held it fast. He became a steadfast seed-sower, bringing forth fruit: "some thirty, some sixty, and some a hundredfold" *(Mark 4:20)*. Paul became a sower.

Kingdom Sowers

What about you? As with Paul, the maturing seed within you emerges as "fruit whose seed is in itself" *(Gen. 1:12)*. Are you willing to become a sower of that kingdom seed? Are you excited to become a bearer of that kingdom fruit? If so, you enjoy privileged joint-participation with all three persons of the Godhead. Can you even imagine? God the Father, God the Son, and God the Holy Spirit invite you and me to participate with them in winning territory for their kingdom. In accepting this challenge, we share with the apostles, early disciples, and with every converted man and woman of faith since then. The profound honor of this opportunity astounds and humbles me. I feel unworthy. I feel unable. I feel insufficient. Perhaps you think this way also. That's "O.K." There is good news: God is worthy *(Rev. 4:11)*. God is able *(Eph. 3:20)*. God is sufficient *(2 Cor. 3:5)*. His "power is made perfect in weakness" *(2 Cor. 12:9)*. Our eternal triune God welcomes women of faith as Kingdom Sowers. Are you willing? God's seed is ready.

Kingdom Synergy

Early Spirit-approved examples demonstrate God's expectation that women should, indeed, participate as sowers of kingdom seed. The letter to the Galatians is addressed to the *adelphoi (Gal. 1:11; 3:15; 4:12, 28, 31; 5:11; 6:1, 18)*. Although the term normally refers to "a male from the same womb as the reference person," i.e., brother, "the plural can also mean brothers and sisters" *(BDAG, 18)*. Accordingly, the familiar biblical word, "brethren," includes both male and female siblings in a family—in this case, brothers and sisters in the family of God.

Paul assigned a special term to persons of faith whose personal goals align with God's purposeful intention: fellow workers, or *sunergos*. So what is a *sunergos*? It is a compound of *sun* *(alongside)* and *ergos* *(worker)*, i.e., an alongside worker. Several hundred years ago, this term entered the English language as synergy, denoting "combined action or operation" of two or more objects to produce a combined effect that is greater than the sum of their separate effects *(Merriam-Webster)*.

Woman of faith, the Lord invites you to become *sunergoi* for the kingdom of God. Are you ready?

Like Phoebe, a *sunergos*, whose noteworthy toil in the early church still encourages and enlivens women of faith today. Phoebe "our sister," as patroness, assisted many *(Rom. 16:1-2)*. Will you generously serve and assist?

Like Priscilla, a *sunergos* *(Rom. 16:3)* who worked alongside her husband, sowing kingdom seed. "They took *(Apollos)* aside and explained the word of God to him more accurately," then "encouraged him and wrote to the disciples to welcome him" in Achaia *(Acts 18:26-27)*. Will you eagerly explain, encourage, and welcome?

Like "those women," *sunergoi*, who labored alongside Paul "in the gospel." Their names are written "in the book of life" *(Phil. 4:3)*. Will you selflessly labor, even when no one except God remembers your name?

Like Junia, a *sunergos* and early convert who labored alongside Andronicus *(assumed to be her husband)*. Junia *(a probable preacher's wife)*, endured imprisonment, encouraged her husband and earned the respect of the apostles *(Rom. 16:7)*. Will you admirably endure and encourage with dignity?

Like Tryphena and Tryphosa, *sunergoi*, *(likely)* twin sisters who labored in Rome *(Rom. 16:12)*. Their names mean "dainty" and "delicate," yet Paul praised them as hearty workers. Will you persistently strengthen yourself in the Lord your God?

Serendipitous Sowing

Last week, our son, Zachary, discovered a flourishing pumpkin patch by the roadside. How did it get there?! Perhaps a near neighbor tossed an old pumpkin? Maybe rain washed chance seed our way? Either way, enthusiastic young hands gathered, carved, and proudly displayed the excellent harvest of chance seed. Seed-sowing produces fruit, whether or not you intend it.

No matter your mindset or stage of life, you are sowing seed. Even incidentally, you are sowing seed. This is like one who scatters the seed in Mark 4:26-29. After scattering the seed, the sower moved on, "sleeping and rising night and day." All the while, "the seed sprouts and grows," but the sower "does not know how." Even unintentional sowing produces fruit, and it is not the sower's job to micromanage details. Those details unfold by God's provision, "first the blade, then the ear, then the full grain." Though you do not understand how, your scattered seed sprouts and grows, producing fruit. How, then, should we sow?

God's Right to Choose

First, We Sow Obediently

The will of our Sovereign God reigns within every woman of true faith, so we delight to do His work in His way. What good would it do to spend energy laboring diligently for God while rejecting His instructions for how He wants it done? I am convinced that every woman reading these words agrees heartily with this rudimentary concept. As women of faith, we enjoy profound privilege as *sunergoi* in the kingdom. As Sovereign King, God enjoys exclusive entitlement to outline how He wants it done, without regard to ever-changing cultural standards. Considering God's right to choose, I invite you to consider a few God-breathed instructions that challenge many Christian women in our American culture.

I permit no woman to teach or have authority over a man, but to be in silence. For Adam was formed first, then Eve; and Adam was not deceived, but the woman was deceived and became a transgressor (1 Tim. 2:12-13).

Wives, in the same way, be submissive to your husbands, so that even if some do not obey the word, they may, without a word, be won by the conduct of their wives, when they observe your chaste conduct, accompanied by reverence (1 Pet. 3:1-2).

As in all the churches of the saints, let your women keep silent in the churches, for they are not permitted to speak, but to be submissive, as the law also says. And if they want to learn something, let them ask their own husbands at home; for it is shameful for women to speak in church (1 Cor. 14:33-35).

I want you to understand that the head of every man is Christ, and the head of woman is man, and the head of Christ is God. Every man praying or prophesying, having his head covered, dishonors his head. But every woman that prays or prophesies with her head uncovered dishonors her head (1 Cor. 11:3-5).

How do you feel when reading these verses? I confess discomfort. I love God's word and desire His reign over my efforts to sow kingdom seed. Yet, I feel discomfort. Why? Because so many loudly scorn these

God-ordained principles. Because these declarations of God stand outside the thinking of contemporary American culture. Because I am not sure that I really know how to be this way myself.

Yes, in every age and society, a genuine faith-walk demands demonstration of unwavering allegiance to God's ways. As each heart soil encounters remnants of a worldly culture, "We ought to obey God rather than man" *(Acts 5:29)*. How is your heart as you read through these verses about God's role assignment for women in the church?

So, what should we do with these concepts? How can we apply God's instructions to the question of female leadership in local worship assemblies? In light of God's right to choose, should women lead the worship in an assembly of both men and women? In light of God's right to choose, should women lead the prayers of a public assembly? In light of God's right to choose, should women publicly direct or oversee the Lord's Supper? In light of God's right to choose, should women perform the public reading of Scripture in a mixed worship assembly?

Instead of allowing the heat of cultural indignation to rise in our hearts, I hope that we choose to decisively, prayerfully, reverently accept these God-breathed words. My prayer is that we consider the context of each teaching, intending to align our will to the will of God. My aim, as a woman of faith, involves making my best effort to do God's work in God's way. So, first of all, we sow obediently.

Next, We Sow Abundantly

Will you sow abundantly for God? Seven years ago, I profusely planted red potatoes, assuming a yield of one potato per sprout. Expecting about forty potatoes, I reached down into the soil at harvest-time. Well! Each sprouted eye produced far more than one new potato! Each sprouted eye produced twenty or more potatoes! Even though it was accidental on my part, reaping 300 potatoes declared undeniably: Abundant sowing yields an abundant harvest. What are you planting for God? Are you continually planting Jesus, the Word, both in yourself and in hearts around you? If you keep planting Jesus, you will richly reap more and more of Him in your life.

Sow Everywhere

Despite extreme physical challenges, Paul, the sower, scattered kingdom seed anywhere he found himself (Gal. 4:13). Despite hardship, the scattered Christians in Acts 8:4 sowed everywhere they happened to be. Surely, there were women included in this number. Can we still do this? Really?

What does this look like tomorrow? ...while you serve breakfast to your family? ...during the drive to school, or homeschool co-op? ...with your colleagues from work? ...over coffee or lunch with your friend? ...waiting on the sidelines for soccer/ basketball/ football/ cross-country practice? ...while volunteering time at a local shelter? ...at your extended family gathering? ...during the doctor appointment? ...at piano/ violin/ guitar/ voice/ drum lessons? ...at the post office/ gas station? ...at the mall/ outlet stores? ...in line at the bank/ the fast food restaurant/ the grocery store? ...while your tires are being rotated? ...over the family dinner table? ... during your family's nighttime routine?

Sow All the Time

Throughout Sacred Scripture, God's directs His people to give *(and keep on giving)*, do *(and keep on doing)*, sow *(and keep on sowing)*. When viewed from a physical *(i.e., fleshly)* perspective, perceived hindrances offer justifications to slow or even cease our giving, doing, and sowing. Solomon explains this principle: "He who observes the wind will not sow, and he who regards the clouds will not reap" *(Eccl. 11:4)*.

We want to focus on God and His ways, sowing kingdom seed everywhere and all the time, but our flesh feels tired. We seek rest. We want to sow kingdom seed in our hearts by worshipping and magnifying God this week. But hormones kick in, allergies, or busyness. We want to sow kingdom seed by opening our hearts and hands to those who are struggling and in need. But sports commitments, my favorite TV show, my hair and nail appointments interfere. Such perceived hindrances dissuade many. Reading through "hormones, allergies, sports, and hair appointments," I am confident that most of us understand the need to press past these challenges and sow kingdom seed anyway. So, many of us do. We press on; we persist; we sow kingdom seed.

Sow Anyway

Then guess what? Often, "hormones, allergies, sports, and hair appointments" give way to "severe chemical imbalance, auto-immune disorder, flood and storm repairs, and oncology appointments." Can you see what happened there? Sowing kingdom seed got harder, not easier. Because it is rarely expected, this reality of harder-not-easier threatens the faith of many kingdom sowers.

So what should we do? In faith, we follow the example of Paul, who was left for dead on the side of the road after sowing kingdom seed. We emulate his example as he rose up and sowed kingdom seed to strangers in Galatia who tended his wounds. To the maximum of our ability, we rise up, sowing the seed to those tending our wounds. With generous hearts and open hands, we rally strength, scattering seed even through the dark and difficult moments. Solomon understood this: "In the morning sow your seed, and in the evening do not withhold your hand, for you do not know which will prosper, either this or that" *(Eccl. 11:6)*; for "you do not know the works of God who does all" *(Eccl. 11:5)*.

Sow anyway. Sow by the hospital bed of a beloved family member. . .as you interact with a hospice nurse. . .when you lose your job, again. . .when you cannot pay the bills this month. . .when your enraged neighbor arrives at the door. . .when the life growing inside you dies before it comes to birth. . .when your heart shatters. . .when hopes die.

Sow Again

Because an enemy attacked and corrupted Paul's gospel planting, he sowed the pure Christ-seed again. "My little children, I am again in the anguish of childbirth, until Christ is formed in you" *(Gal. 4:19)*. Sowing the seed of the kingdom is never just "once-and-done," not even when you have sown abundantly.

Sometimes, second sowing is necessary. Enemies, troublers, and corrupting influences notice the growth of Christ-seed in you, in your family, in your community. They notice, then relentlessly assault, just as they did in Galatia. So then what? Sow again. Sometimes, a second/third/fourth sowing is necessary "until Christ is formed" in us. Sow again.

Conclusion

Paul became a sower. Once the Word took root in the fertile field of Saul's heart, that seed grew and developed, transforming his will and actions *(Gal. 1-2)*. Questioning his "conversion," most Christians just shut him out. Because of his "out of season" call to apostleship, other church leaders hesitantly awaited clarifying results. Physically, he often felt like a burden. Spiritually, he anguished over the fruit of his labor. Confronting these challenges *(and many more)* required patient continuance. Despite harsh impediments, Paul actively chose Jesus the Word, sowing seed for God. What about you? *Whatever it takes, get the seed to the soil.*

Thought Questions

1. What's Your Story? Like Paul, each of us has a story. What's yours?

2. Enter Your Name Here: _____, the sinner.

3. Enter Your Name Here: _____, the field.

4. Enter Your Name Here: _____, the sower.

5. According to Galatians 3: 16, how did God bring His seed among humanity?

6. According to Galatians 3:29, what do we become once we belong to Christ?

7. According to Galatians 3:27, who are those who belong to Christ?

8. According to Galatians 3:25, what has now come?

9. According to Galatians 3:24, how are we justified? What advantages does a living word have over other books of religious wisdom and instruction? Christ?

10. Paul penned this letter "to the churches of Galatia" *(Gal. 1:2)*. Were there any women in Galatia?

11. Were there any women in other churches at that time? How do you know?

12. In the New Testament record, in what ways were women involved in sowing gospel seed?

13. Do you think God intends the same kinds of activity for women of faith today? Why or why not?

14. According to 1 Peter 1:23, what is God's seed?

15. According to John 1:1-14, what *(or who)* is the Word?

16. According to Romans 10:17, what does the word produce?

17. According to Hebrews 4:12, what characteristic of the word enables it to produce anything?

18. In your own words, explain the identity and purpose of God's seed among humanity.

Concept Seeds

To begin preparation for the next lesson, please consider the following question:

In your own words, try to express what you know about the Holy Spirit. What verses guide your answer?

Spirit-Seed in Galatia

Lesson 3: Introduction

The word of God is the treasure. The heart of humans is the field. Less than twenty years after Jesus's resurrection, this treasure of God, hidden in the heart of Paul, arrived in Galatia.

We have this treasure in earthen vessels (2 Cor. 4:7).

Resulting in a true knowledge of God's mystery, that is, Christ Himself, in whom are hidden all the treasures of wisdom and knowledge (Col. 2:3).

Forty-Eight Hours to Survive

After germination, seeds have forty-eight hours to survive. Seeds transmit life through metamorphosis. This time of transformation *(i.e., from a hardy, encapsulated, guarded seed to a fragile seedling)* is a vulnerable time. Embryonic possibility and survival provision exist inside every seed. Germination will not even begin unless there are sufficient internal stores of nutrients and energy to ensure at least short-term survival. Once germination starts, that embryo's opportunity begins. Inside the seed, there is found a reservoir of food needed to power initial seedling growth. After forty-eight hours, that internal power source depletes,

leaving the seedling to access sources of light, water, and nutrition outside itself.

Spirit-Seed

In the letter to Galatia, Paul makes one primary point about the seed that gives birth to Christ-like creatures: it is Spirit, not flesh. But, what is "Spirit"? The concept of "spirit" is foundational to understanding all biblical principles, and especially to understanding Paul's letter to the Christ-like ones in Galatia. Beginning on the first page of the Divine Record, Spirit is present. "The Spirit of God was hovering over the face of the waters" *(Gen. 1:2)*. Again, on the last page of the Divine Record, Spirit is present. "The Spirit and the Bride say, 'Come'" *(Rev. 22:17)*. From the beginning to the end, Spirit is present, active, and involved in deity's mission of revelation, invitation, and salvation. So, we cannot ignore Spirit. It is foundational. The seed that brings forth Christ-like creatures is not flesh. The seed that brings forth Christians is Spirit-seed.

Definition

The Greek word for "spirit" is *pneuma*, from the verb *pneō*, meaning to breathe, or blow. *Pneuma* is something that breathes or blows forth unseen. The Holy Spirit *(hagios pneuma)*, the third person of the Godhead,

is described to humans as the Holy Breath blowing forth from God. That is not to say that the Holy Spirit is only breath, but God uses something as simple as breath *(or wind)* to describe the unseen nature of this member of His three-fold make-up. The Holy Breath *(i.e. the Holy Spirit)* from God is eternal and it is life.

Loss of Breath Is Death

The spirit-breath given to Adam came from God's Holy Breath. Adam was not made a god, but he shared the image of His Holy Breath. God's Holy Breath is sacred and pure; it cannot coexist with sin. So, when we sin, we corrupt the nature and purpose of our own spirit-breath and destroy our relationship with the One who is Holy Breath. God's Holy Breath cannot share *(i.e., have fellowship or abide)* with us anymore.

This happened to Adam and Eve. They lost fellowship with the eternal, life-giving Holy Breath. They still had temporal flesh-life for a while, but their spirit-breath from God's Holy Breath was corrupted. Their open relationship with God ended when they sinned. Just as Adam and Eve were driven from the garden, and no longer shared fellowship with Him after they sinned, God's Holy Breath cannot remain in fellowship with our spirit-breath when we sin. This is death. This is spiritual death—the separation of our spirit from God's Spirit.

This cannot be fixed by any human means. As long as sin clings to us, God's Holy Breath cannot have fellowship with us.

Gift of Breath Is Life

Praise God, who made a way to restore fellowship between His Holy Breath and the tainted spirits of sinful humanity. God Himself brought about the possibility for our salvation *(Isa. 59:16)*. God spent several thousand years preparing a new and living way to reunite His Holy Breath *(which brings eternal life)* with the flesh-animating life-force and spirit-breath of humanity. He provided a pure, sinless, holy Human so that His pure, sinless, Holy Breath could inhabit flesh in that body. He provided His own Son, Jesus, for our salvation. Conquering sin in the person of Jesus

Christ, He provides a path of redemption to lost humanity, desiring to restore fellowship between His Holy Breath and humanity.

When we are born into His holy body, we share again fellowship with the Holy Breath of God. Our spirit renews its likeness to God's Spirit. God's Spirit is eternal. It is life. "Then Peter said to them, 'Repent, and let every one of you be baptized in the name of Jesus Christ for the remission of sins; and you shall receive the gift of the Holy Spirit *(hagios pneuma, i.e., Holy Breath)'*" *(Acts 2:38)*. Those who are baptized for the remission of sins *(born of water)* receive the gift of Holy Breath *(born of Spirit)*. God's Spirit brings eternal life to our spirit. What amazing love!

How Does One Receive the Gift?

How did the disciples in Galatia receive this great gift? How did they receive this Spirit? "By hearing with faith," not by works of the law *(Gal. 3:2)*. How did they begin as Christ-like creatures? "Having begun by the Spirit" *(3:3)*. How were they growing toward completion? By the Spirit, not the flesh *(3:3)*. How was the Spirit supplied to the Galatians? "By hearing with faith," not by works of the law *(3:5)*. How were miracles working among them? "By hearing with faith," not by works of the law *(3:5)*. How did the promised Spirit come to the Gentiles? "Through faith" *(3:14)*. Where did the promised Spirit come to the Gentiles? "In Christ Jesus" *(3:14)*. How can we expect the "hope of righteousness"? "Through the Spirit, by faith" *(5:5)*.

How Does One Live with the Gift?

In his book *How Does the Holy Spirit Work in a Christian?*, commenting on the command, "If we live in the Spirit, let us also walk in the Spirit," from Galatians 5:25, Kyle Pope explains it this way:

There is clearly an aspect of the work of the Holy Spirit which is God's part, but there is also a part which is dependent upon (each person's) choice. When one is obedient to the gospel, the restoration of man unto God involves the Holy Spirit. Paul calls this living "in the Spirit" (Gal. 5:25). Yet, Paul also shows there is an aspect of yielding to the Spirit which is (each person's) choice. One must "walk in the Spirit" (Gal. 5:16). Paul teaches, "If

we live in the Spirit, let us also walk in the Spirit" (Gal. 5:25). In this sense one is to "be filled with the Holy Spirit"—a command (Eph. 5:18). We must sow to the Spirit in order to reap of the Spirit eternal life (Gal. 6:8) (39).

How can we live with this great gift? The same way as did the Galatian disciples. How can we "not gratify the desires of the flesh"? As we "walk by the Spirit" *(Gal. 5:16)*. Can we keep fulfilling the desires of the flesh, and also fulfill the desires of the Spirit? No. "These are opposed to each other" *(5:17)*. How can we live "not under law"? "If you are led by the Spirit" *(5:18)*. How do we live once we are in the body of Christ Jesus? "Crucify the flesh and its passions and desires" *(5:25)*. How do we live by the Spirit? "Keep in step with the Spirit" *(5:25)*. What fruit results in those born of Spirit-seed? "Love, joy, peace, patience, kindness, goodness, faithfulness, gentleness, self-control" *(5:22-23)*. What will we reap by sowing to the Spirit? "Eternal life" *(6:8)*. Paul sowed Spirit-seed *(not flesh-seed)* in Galatia, which produced Christians. Redeemed from sin, and added to His body, Christians, *(i.e., Christ-like ones)* partake of God's Holy Breath as we feed upon the revelation that comes from His revealed word. Although we do not yet perceive eternal life, faith establishes hope. Seeing the unseen, we walk by faith, which produces Spirit-fruit. Disciples of Christ are identifiable when they produce Spirit-fruit: "You will know them by their fruits" *(Matt. 7:16)*.

Spirit-Seed Traits

Living Seed

In producing Christ-like creatures, the living word cuts and pierces, divides and discerns *(Heb. 4:12)*. This word is not lifeless markings on a decorative book page. This word lives, animated by dynamic power *(Rom. 1:16)*, and apt to drastically transform you from flesh *(which is dead because of sin)* to Spirit *(which is life because of righteousness) (Rom. 8:10)*. "For to be fleshly minded *is* death, but to be spiritually minded *is* life and peace" *(Rom. 8:6)*. The results depend on you. How do you receive this living seed, the word of God?

Incorruptible Seed

Spirit-seed is incorruptible. Abiding within the safety of God's will demonstrates a life submitted to God's living word. In Him, we rest in hope. "Now hope does not disappoint, because the love of God has been poured out in our hearts by the Holy Spirit who was given to us" *(Rom. 5:5)*. In Him, we enjoy soundness instead. "Soundness" denotes wholeness and health, ideally of body, soul, spirit, and mind *(1 Thess. 5:23)*. Those who are sound live in Christ, as the body of Christ, forgiven and uncorrupted. "In Christ, we who are many are one body" *(Rom. 12:5)*. Those born of incorruptible seed live uncorrupted lives, cleansed from all sin by the blood of Jesus Christ. "If we confess our sins, He is faithful and just to forgive us our sins" *(1 John 1:7-9)*. Does this describe your life today? Have you escaped sin-sickness? Are you sound and uncorrupted? As women of faith, we all strive towards this description. Each day we put away a little more sin. Each day we grow a little more in Christ. As long as we live, we press towards this goal of living in agreement with the incorruptible Spirit-seed.

Implanted Seed

Spirit-seed, planted in our hearts, saves us, but only if we "receive with meekness the implanted word" *(Jas. 1:21)*. God, the Father, sows the good and incorruptible seed, intending for it to accomplish a particular work. However, this implanted word, the seed, will not flourish in you against your own will.

Transforming Seed

Spirit-seed transforms us from death to life, containing inherent remodeling power *(Rom. 1:16)*. Transformation occurs as you manifestly submit your life, day by day, and piece by piece to this Seed within you, allowing it to overrun and replace seeds and weeds of the old you.

Spirit-Seed Results

Transformed Hearts

Moment by moment, Spirit-seed transforms us from the inside out. This occurs in the inner man. While in transformation, some time may pass during which only scant evidence of this inward change is visible. Jesus explained why it happens like this: "It is like leaven, which a woman took and hid in three pecks of flour until it was all leavened"

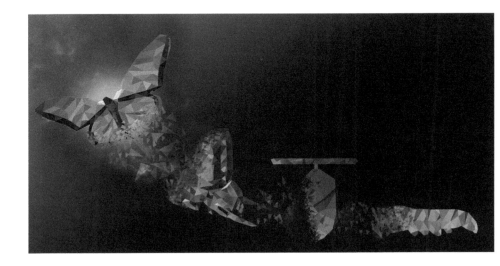

(Luke 13:21; Matt. 13:33). Thus, the reign of the Christ-life within each Christian is the seed, the kingdom of God, multiplying like leaven in a lump of dough until it accomplishes a complete transformation.

Abraham's (Flesh) Seed

God demonstrated this process with the seed of Abraham. His great-grandson, Joseph, ascended by God's providence to power in Egypt. From his position of power, he offered protection to the family of Abraham's grandson, Jacob. Thus, the *(flesh)* seed of Abraham in seventy persons was hidden, like leaven, in Goshen in Egypt. Hidden and protected in that place, the *(flesh)* seed of Abraham multiplied until the process of leavening was complete. As God had promised, after 400 years, the multiplied seed was ready to stand on its own. What began as one man, Abraham, became seventy persons. Those seventy persons multiplied into millions. Then God said they were ready, and He set about to bring them out from Egypt.

Abraham's (Spirit) Seed

Now, this same process is happening again, but this time in human heart soil, not Egyptian soil. "For behold, the kingdom of God is within you" *(Luke 17:21).* Now, the *(Spirit)* Seed of Abraham multiplies as hidden leaven in every receptive human heart soil. Pliable hearts are transformed by this Seed's power. Willing minds regenerate. Inner selves renew. Paul said, "Do not be conformed to this world but be transformed by the renewing of your mind, so that you may prove what is that good and acceptable and perfect will of God" *(Rom. 12:2)*. The Seed of promise, which is Christ *(Gal. 3:16, 29)*, increases in willing hearts until it fully takes over those who have yielded control.

Transformed Lives

"It is no longer I who live, but Christ lives in me" *(Gal. 2:20)*. When Jesus dwells in us, "The body is dead because of sin, but the spirit is life because of righteousness" *(Rom. 8:10)*. For this reason, we no longer live, walk, talk, or even think according to the flesh. Why? Because the flesh is dead. Day by day, as we resolutely seek Christ, external evidence of internal change increases.

Experiencing this profound hope, I think of Mary Magdalene. By His powerful Word, Jesus cast seven demons out of Mary Magdalene *(Luke 8:2)*. From that moment forward, all history witnesses her transformation. Taking advantage of opportunities to see and hear Lord Jesus continually, Mary traveled along as "He went on through cities and villages, proclaiming and bringing the good news of the kingdom of God" *(Luke 8:1)*. As the earth quaked, and the heavens darkened at Jesus's death, Mary observed first-hand *(Matt. 27:56)*. Hours later, Jesus retained preeminence for her, as she followed His body, seating herself by His tomb *(Matt. 27:61)*. Because Mary diligently redeemed every moment attending her Lord, He richly rewarded her. On resurrection day, as soon as the sun had risen *(Mark 16:2)*, Jesus, "appeared first to Mary Magdalene" *(Mark 16:9)*, even as she sought Him, weeping *(John 20:13)*. As Jesus, the Incarnate Word, transformed Mary's destiny, He can transform your destiny!

Transformed Destinies

In the flesh, sin reigns, confining destinies to eternal separation from the life of God. In the flesh, we are death-bound, separated from God's

Holy Breath. "That which is born of flesh is flesh" *(John 3:6)*. In Spirit, Christ reigns, opening destinies to eternal oneness in the life of God. In Christ, we are life-bound, born again of water and the Spirit. "That which is born of Spirit is spirit" *(John 3:7)*. Spirit-seed transforms us from spiritual death to eternal life.

I am reminded of an unnamed New Testament disciple and her purposeful encounter with Christ. Identified principally as "the woman with the issue of blood" *(Mark 5:25; Matt. 9:20; Luke 8:43)*, she desperately needed Christ. Being ceremonially unclean for twelve years *(Num. 19:20)* condemned her to extended loneliness and isolation. Passing from doctor to doctor, seeking answers, but finding none, she experienced futile suffering until her money and hope were gone. Then she learned about Jesus. Her interaction at the feet of Jesus surprises me. How did she "pull" the power from Jesus, so that He felt it go out from Him *(Mark 5:28-30)*? I cannot fully understand what she experienced. Yet I know the strength of her faith compelled her to reach out. Hoping in the power of Jesus, she was rewarded: no longer unseen, but seen; no longer unclean, but clean. What about you? Do you desperately need Christ?

Conclusion

The human heart is soil; the word is the seed *(John 1:1; 1 Pet. 1:23)*. Germination of this seed within us transforms guarded, worldly creatures into fragile seedlings in Christ. During this vulnerable time, every newly born Christian contains enough internal storage of power and spiritual nutrition to survive for at least a short time. This means every new spiritual seedling—every one of us—starts with a fair chance of survival. After our internal reserves deplete, God provides access to the source of light, water, and bread, for those who decidedly pursue it. Thankfully, God allows spiritual seedlings more than forty-eight hours!

Thought Questions

1. In your own words, describe how the seed of God transforms from the inside out.

2. Why does it matter that the Word is "living"? Give at least two reasons.

3. From the Galatian letter, describe the relationship between Spirit and flesh.

4. From the Galatian letter, describe the changes that occur once the heart receives the implanted Word.

5. From your understanding of the Bible, how would you define death?

6. How does the definition of Spirit as breath aid your conception of the Holy Spirit?

7. Define incorruptible.

8. Can you think of two more biblical examples of transformed lives or destinies?

9. Define living.

10. What advantages does a living word have over other books of religious wisdom and instruction?

Concept Seeds

To begin preparation for the next lesson, please consider the following question:

Do you think women of faith should openly, mercifully interact with people who practice works of the flesh? If so, what verses would you use to explain your answer? If not, what verses would you use to support your answer?

Flesh-Seed in Galatia

Lesson 4: Introduction

In 1999, rotting fruit was on sale. At an open-air market in Vilnius, Lithuania, a wrinkled woman pedaled half-eaten, rotting fruit, without regard to its stench or decay. At the end of a row of vendors, in a non-existent stall, the gaudy, pink shawl insufficiently protected her against Arctic November winds. Approaching hesitantly, I wondered at the feverish glaze of borderline insanity in those unseeing, far-seeing eyes. Shifting distrustfully, she acknowledged my presence by a flicker of hesitation, then slowly stepped away, lowering her prices for a less curious passerby. This actually happened! She was selling rotting fruit . . .with bites taken out of it.

What do you think I should have done for this woman with her decaying, rotting fruit? Honestly, the scene astounded me then and haunts me to the point of chills even now. Yet, I learned some things. I learned some sad things.

Flesh-seed's fruit dies, then corrupts. Corruption is ruin and decay. Corruption is stench and rottenness. Corruption is fetid food for larvae, maggots, worms, rats, and birds of prey. This pervasive reality of death-then-decay sobers me, and I learn. Serving sin with my flesh produces this same ruin and rot. Flesh dies. Then it decays, becoming corrupt.

Corruptible Seed

There are only two choices, Spirit or flesh. We cannot mix the two. Around AD 46, two seeds were being sown in Galatia. Paul, the sower, shared Jesus Christ, the Word, in Galatia. Close behind him, troublers sowed a different gospel. What do you think of as you hear this term, "a different gospel" *(Gal. 1:6)*? That sounds dramatic to me. I think most of us would consider "a different gospel" to be vastly different teaching. To modern American Christian women, "a different gospel" might include some of the following:

- They might believe in a different god than Yahweh, such as those who worship Allah, Buddha, Brahman, or the dual god, Lady Diana, and Lord Pan.

- They might follow a different savior than Jesus Christ the Son of God, such as accepting Jesus Christ as a mere prophet but not One equal with God, or saving self by following the Noble Eightfold Path to Nirvana, or saving self by the path of personal preference *(either through works, knowledge, or devotion)*; or salvation through continual reincarnation until one ends in "the Summerland" *(a.k.a. Elysian Fields, Valhalla, or Hades)*.

- They might adhere to a different moral standard than the life and teaching of Christ, such as the Qur'an, or the Five Precepts of Buddhism, or Dharma, or the Rule of Three.

- They might participate in a different set of religious practices than the Spirit-approved practices of the New Testament church, such

as the Five Pillars of Islam, the Eight Steps to Enlightenment in Buddhism, the Sanskrit Vedas of Hinduism, or the Charge of the Goddess for Wicca.

Surprisingly, though, the "different gospel" confronted by Paul in Galatia approached none of these extremes. Christians who were turning aside to a different gospel still worshipped Yahweh as God. They still believed in Jesus Christ as the Son of God. They seemed to desire righteous lives like Christ and followed the teachings of the apostles *(as is evident in Galatians 2)*. So what was the problem? The problem was only one thing. The problem was only one change. The problem was binding circumcision as necessary for salvation. Just one thing, leftover from their pre-conversion convictions, initiated Paul's astonishment. "I am astonished that you are so quickly deserting him who called you in the grace of Christ and are turning to a different gospel. . . If anyone is preaching to you a gospel contrary to the one you received, let him be accursed *(anathema)*" *(Gal. 1:6, 9)*. There are only two choices: the gospel of Christ *(Spirit)* or a different gospel *(flesh)*. Not even one thing can be mixed or leftover. We can only choose one. What do you choose? Flesh or Spirit?

Sowing to the Flesh Has Its Rewards

Flesh produces an immediate, apparent, external reward. It promises instant gratification, and satisfying rewards—all of which feed the lust of the flesh, the lust of the eyes, and the pride of life. For Jewish leaders in Galatia, binding where God had not bound *(i.e., circumcision as necessary for salvation)*, gratified the pride of life. They felt elevated. They felt righteous. They felt right.

If sin brought no reward, then no one would ever sow to the flesh. Yet, the universal human truth is that we have all sown to the flesh, choosing the immediate reward of sin over the eternal reward of sowing to the Spirit.

The rewards of the flesh last a moment, a day, a week. Fleeting satiation promptly gives way to more need, more desire, more want. It is never enough. This truth about fleshly reward applies to every "category," including sexual sin, religious sin, heart sin, and self-control sin. Although this goal of immediate reward manifests with sexual sin or self-control sin, the same objective also foundationally promotes religious sin and heart sin.

Sowing to the Flesh Is Obvious

"For he who sows to the flesh shall of the flesh reap corruption" *(Gal. 6:8)*. This phrase, "sowing to the flesh," literally expresses sowing or scattering for one's own flesh, or to please one's own flesh. So what does that mean in daily life? What would it look like on a Monday morning for you to "sow for pleasing your own flesh"? Well, some things are apparent, or, as Paul expressed it, the works for one's own flesh are "evident" *(5:19)*.

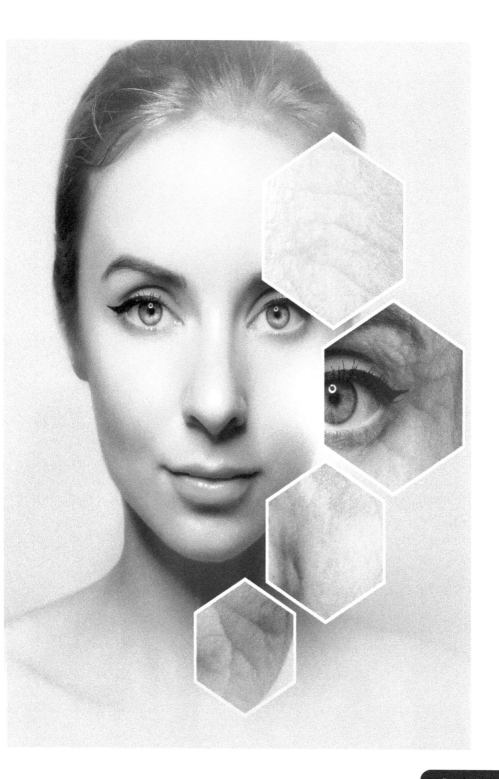

Definitions

Here is a defined list from Galatians 5:19-21 of these obvious actions for pleasing one's own flesh:

Sexual immorality *(porneia)* is a work of the flesh that includes a wide variety of self-satisfying sexual conduct outside the marriage bed.

Impurity *(akatharsia)* is a work of the flesh that is even broader than *porneia*. Porneia refers to sexual action, but impurity is general sexual uncleanness, including perverted sexual thoughts, illicit sexual excitement through filthy language, suggestive words and behaviors, viewing pornographic pictures or videos, enticing others toward sexual action with suggestive flirtation and flattery, etc. Any language or behavior that encourages and supports sexual impropriety is impurity.

Sensuality *(aselgeia)* is a work of the flesh that satisfies self in much the same way as impurity. The difference between the two seems to hinge on attitude and degree. Sensuality is flagrant and shameless. People practicing the sin of sensuality will be loud, proud, and in your face with their sin.

Idolatry *(eidololatria)* is a work of the flesh that finds expression in worshipping the product of your own imaginations and appetites. Idolatry focuses desire and hope into the products designed and crafted in the worshipper's own mind, or by the worshipper's own hand.

Sorcery *(pharmakeia)* is a work of the flesh involving the consumption of drugs that historically were part of occult practices—to get high, to escape hard realities, or to pursue "enlightenment." The concept also includes associated practices of witchcraft, spells, curses, and using illicit drugs to enhance the perceived effect of the sorcery. On one level, we may think of entry-level sorcery as palm reading, fortune-telling, astrology, or channeling. Commonly, many in our culture travel much deeper into the dark arts, participating in outright drug use, witchcraft, and sorcery, portraying this work of flesh as a valid religious and lifestyle choice.

Enmity *(echthrai)*, a work of the flesh, manifests itself as hatred, bitterness, ill-will, and, generally, an enemy mindset. As we witness with Cain at the dawn of humanity, full-grown enmity is murder.

Strife *(eris)*, a work of the flesh, is often the first outward evidence that enmity resides in the heart. Strife produces discord, tension, quarreling, attacking. Strife disrupts unity and replaces it with adversarial outlook and treatment.

Jealousy *(zēlos)*, as work of the flesh, refers to ardent, zealous resentment towards real or perceived inequities of material, intellectual, appearance, or even spiritual blessing. Sinful jealousy grows from covetousness, and traps the one practicing it in a constant state of torment. Jealousy practices indignation against what others have, but do not "deserve."

Fits of anger *(thumos)*, as a work of the flesh, describes a temperament marked by explosive anger with uncontrolled outbursts and attacks. Fits of anger, or wrath, deeply wound both the intentional and unintentional targets, destroying trust and love.

Rivalries *(eritheia)*, a work of the flesh, describe actions and words of self-interested people who create warring factions to feed their ego, agenda, and advancement.

Dissensions *(dichostasia)*, a work of the flesh, when practiced within the church, segregates the unified body of Christ into pieces. Social, racial, educational, opinion-based, or even doctrinally-based dissensions create distrust rather than mutual edification among brothers and sisters in the body of Christ.

Divisions *(hairesis)*, a work of the flesh, exists as the residue of rivalries and dissensions. These divisions, or heresies, devastate, leaving pieces of Christ's body lost, broken, isolated, degraded, scorned, or mocked.

Envy *(phthonos)*, a work of the flesh, directs ardent, zealous hatred towards one who possesses what is desired. Envy attacks the materially, intellectually, beautifully, or spiritually prosperous with cutting looks, hateful words, and ignoble actions.

Drunkenness *(methē)*, a work of the flesh, involves intoxication. One's intellectual, physical, and moral capacities are compromised from the inebriating effects of substances taken into the body. This includes alcohol, and other habit-forming substances which produce the same effect.

Orgies *(kōmos)*, a work of the flesh, occurs as excessive, uninhibited feeding and satisfying of one's flesh with full indulgence in drugs, alcohol, lusts, and lewdness.

And things like these *(toutois homoios)*, i.e., more works of the flesh, include every action that follows the same self-centered, flesh-satisfying impulse as those specifically mentioned. Every Christian can figure out if an action is a work of the flesh. "These are evident" *(Gal. 5:19)*. Their goal is the satisfaction of one's own body and desires, rather than the fulfillment of God's desires.

How do you feel as you read through this list of definitions of the works of flesh? To be honest, I dislike reading it. Several of these works seem extreme. All of them feel embarrassing, base, and negative. Physically, this list initiates a sick disgust, much like the stench from rotting garbage and putrefying fruit. I would prefer to believe that a list like this is unnecessary for Christians, and especially for Christian women. Yet, I wonder, did Paul write this list in the Galatian letter because he thought none of these sins ever had or ever would tempt those Christians? Did the Holy Spirit include this list in the written revelation because He thought no Christian ever had, or ever would, commit any of these sins? Then as now, sin is pervasive and powerful. So, let's be real.

Sexual Sins: Sexual Immorality, Impurity, Sensuality

Sexual immorality, impurity, and sensuality surround and engulf the culture of women of faith in our country. The world's portrayal and packaging of sexuality is anything but moral. In woeful country ballads, upbeat pop tunes, or even while singing the blues, the message of modern music enthrones emotional, sexual love as the height of human experience. Television promotes the same idea, but with the powerful punch of visual portrayal. Where else do we see it? Magazines, expertly woven popular fiction novels, and Hollywood all unite to reinvent and redefine all forms of sexual immorality, impurity, and sensuality. Hollywood serves it up in nationwide 3-D, but we need not look that far. Sensuality is everywhere: walking through malls and parking lots, sitting on bleachers at football games, and tragically, sometimes on the pews during Sunday worship. Every woman of faith today battles this cultural craze to moralize *(and normalize)* sexual immorality, but this is not a new problem.

Ritual Sexuality

In Galatia, Paul sowed the gospel seed in the hearts of people outside the nation of Israel. Known as the Gauls, these Celtic tribes inhabiting Galatia practiced polytheistic worship of ancient tribal gods and goddesses. Several of their ritual feasts included sexual acts, parading sensuality. The anticipation of a new year, or celebration of an old year, often involved sexual immorality. Praying for rain, or enhancing the fertility of crops, often incorporated sensuality in the fields. Blessing a hunt, or protecting a river, often celebrated sexual expression *(Macculough)*. Converted Gentiles in Galatia crucified these sexual works of the flesh but still needed to hear Paul's warning.

Illicit Sexuality

In Galatia, Paul sowed the gospel seed in the hearts of his countrymen. Known as Jews, these Israelite tribes historically practiced monotheistic worship of Yahweh Elohim, who is One *(Deut. 6:4)*. None of their appointed feasts or celebrations involved sexually immoral activity. Nevertheless, from the days of Abraham until the first century, sexual sin also beset Israelites. In Sodom, and later in Gibeah, violent homosexual abusers plagued city inhabitants and unwitting travelers *(Gen. 19:5-7; Judg. 19:22-25)*. In Shiloh, worthless sons of Eli, the High Priest, engaged in sexual immorality. In the place constructed to house holy worshippers of a Holy God, these men committed lewdness and adultery with female tabernacle workers *(1 Sam. 2:22)*. In Israel, Yahweh stated His case against both men and women, young and old, for idolatrous harlotry, shameless adultery, and defiling prostitution at the temple *(Hos. 4:13-14)*. Converted Jews in Galatia crucified these sexual works of the flesh, but a reminder warning was necessary. Whether then or now, Paul emphasizes, "Those who practice such things will not inherit the kingdom of God" *(Gal. 5:21)*.

Religious Sins: Idolatry and Sorcery

"Human history is the long terrible story of man trying to find something other than God which will make him happy"—C.S. Lewis, *Mere Christianity*.

Idolatry is not dead just because the little golden statues declined in popularity. An idol is any person, place, thing, or idea that competes against the essence and position of our exalted God. Constructed by humans, idols boldly deny any dependence on God. Replacing the hope, desire, and will of God with one's own hope, desire, and will showcase pride and self-reliance. What threatens God's supremacy in your life? Although idolatry and sorcery intertwine and overlap in a seemingly inextricable web, all aspects exist under the umbrella of "paganism," i.e., the religious practices of those who are unenlightened.

Judge Not?

What is your judgment of these "unenlightened" idolaters who dare exalt a power other than God the Father, and our Lord Jesus Christ? Does their approach strike you as unreasonable and unsubstantiated? It strikes me that way. At least it once did. Yet, who am I? I am sitting here, comfortably reclined in my living room, several Bible translations within easy reach. I know Yahweh Elohim's account of His re-entry into a world overturned and overrun by Satan. I know about the adversarial accuser who rules this age. I know the history of Israel, a nation through which God *(El)* contends *(Isra)*. I know how God reasserts dominion, bringing forth His conquering One, my Lord Jesus Christ. I know how it all ends. Thus, my perspective quickly dismisses the pagan mindset as ridiculous and unfounded. Maybe this describes your general reaction as well. If so, I invite you into a more compassionate consideration of those "whose minds the god of this age has blinded, who do not believe, lest the light of the gospel of the glory of Christ, who is the image of God, should shine on them" *(2 Cor. 4:4)*.

For millennia, "the nations" undeniably witnessed "the eternal power and Godhead," clearly cognizant of deity's invisible attributes in the created world *(Rom. 1:20)*. Millions groped for understanding, and along the way, constructed systems of religious activity that were based upon God's observable powers. Although the nations possessed no collected revelation from God, intense seeking disclosed some apparent truths. Typical components of pagan religiosity include some of the following:

- **Trinity.** As early as 6000 BC *(according to radiocarbon dating)*, Anatolian worshippers esteemed a triple deity as the creator.
- **Temple.** Deities meet with humanity in designated venues, enjoying and partaking of worshipper's praise, accolades, and gifts.
- **Priesthood.** Ancient Sumerian and Hittite theology included priests and priestesses, who served at the place of worship. Thus

far, "high priest," as a literary term, has not been identified in their languages, but the local king maintained authority over the serving priesthood.

- **Servant-Master Paradigm.** Throughout history, the relationship of man to deity involves rendering service to please and gain favor.

- **Sin.** Fundamental ethical and moral codes ubiquitously populate all pagan traditions.

- **Sacrifice.** Sin is never acceptable and must be answered by sacrifice.

- **Confession.** Sin cannot be hidden or trapped inside but must be acknowledged and confessed.

- **Reciprocity.** Reciprocity, or sowing and reaping, foundationally guides all moral behavior.

- **Death.** Humans die, but gods do not.

- **Afterlife.** Death for humans is only bodily, but "consciousness" continues like the gods.

Wow! This is perceptive, considering they had no Bible, no written revelation from God, and no relationship with the One true God as did ancient Israel. How do you think "the nations" so ably constructed these elements of relationship and religion—even before Yahweh stepped in through Abraham's family to contend, clarify, and regulate? Even the nations *(goyim)*—now termed "Gentiles" in Latin-based languages—sought and perceived aspects of God's prescribed order and authority. Throughout the millennia, pagans incontrovertibly "knew God" *(Rom. 1:21)*.

So how did this conceptual clarity degrade so rapidly into the debauchery, confusion, and chaos of historical heathenry? The reigning adversary of the true, living, Creator presented immediate, self-satisfying options, and the people made their choice. "They did not glorify *Him* as God, nor were thankful, but became futile in their thoughts, and their foolish hearts were darkened. Professing to be wise, they became fools, and changed the glory of the incorruptible God into an image made like corruptible man—and birds and four-footed animals and creeping things" *(Rom. 1:21-22)*.

Humanity chose the god of what is dead. Mortals preferred the god who speaks false, easy things. Idolatry was thus born.

The gods of Gaul

In Galatia, the gods of Gaul threatened Christ's reign in Christian hearts, as worshippers fell prey to the adversary's deceptive lure. The multiplicity of both Celtic and Roman gods surrounded them. Archaeological remains from the area reveal the ram as a customary offering to appease the "strong shades," or dead heroes of families, cities, or tribes. During such feasting, human sacrifices replaced the ram, satisfying underworld gods, and feeding local ghosts. By the first century, Celtic worship traditions undergirding the region's customs already dated back thousands of years. The adversary's hold was not easily broken, even among those actively repenting, turning toward, and chasing after God's Conquering Son.

The Goddess of Wicca

Today, many of the same traditions maintain an enduring, residual influence throughout the world, including America. In 2018, the Pew Research Center revealed that 1.5 million people in America actively follow the same "pre-Christian traditions" as ancient worshippers in Gaul. Their new name is Wicca; they elevate "the goddess" above other gods, goddesses, and spirits; but most holidays and practices remain unchanged. Idolatrous influences, deeply interlaced with sorcery and the cult of the dead, attracted both Jews and Gentiles in the first century. Resurrected today, gods of Gaul still powerfully entice millions *(Zilber)*.

Tyr and Odin, gods of the North

Besides Wicca, several other pre-Christian religious heritages hold sway among us, under their chosen umbrella title, "Heathenry." Within heathenry, common types and components remain uniform and include idolatrous beliefs and practices spanning time and cultures. In America, "The Northern Tradition," or ancient Norse religion, rises as the primary, popular heathen creed. Tyr *(a.k.a. Tyre?)*, the long time ruler of their pantheon, capitulated to Odin after losing his right hand. Odin *(a.k.a. Sidon?)*, their chief god, rules in Asgard. Like me, you may find yourself surprisingly familiar with some of these names. What sounds like innocent caricatures to us, guides the hearts and minds of heathens, and unsuspecting youth, across our country and around the world.

Even So

Insufficient Idol

Idols deceive. Idolatry promises and *(sometimes)* supplies completion, fullness, and security. Yet, its promises are fleeting and false. Up front, idolatry presents its gifts as easy to acquire, costing very little. Idolatry offers everything we want, right now, with little effort. Permissive, fallible gods provide a conduit for legitimizing sin, while still enjoying the privilege of their favor. Yet, the idol's gifts disappear in a moment, leaving behind residual emptiness, death, stench, and rot. Idols deceptively show an ability to mimic God's all-sufficiency, but it is a lie.

All-Sufficient God

"As for God, His way is perfect. The word of the Lord proves true" *(2 Sam. 22:31)*. God promises and supplies lasting completion, fullness, and security. Up front, God presents His reward as difficult to attain, costing much. God's prize is a "pearl of great price," a "hidden treasure," causing such encompassing joy that people give up everything else to have it. This holy, perfect God mercifully provides a conduit, or way, for the forgiveness of sins, through the blood of His Own Son. "While we were yet sinners," God reached for us through His Gift. The offerings and promises of God endure eternally, emerging from His unfailing abundance. He completes and fills His people, who become the fragrance and aroma of Christ. As for God, He is all-sufficient, and His ways are true.

Self-Control Sins

We all understand that every sin derives either from lack of self-control, or outright favor of self-will. In Galatia, Paul's "works of the flesh" enumeration uniformly categorize every "level" of sin, condemning unrestrained negative thought alongside untamed speech and unrestricted feeding of every fleshly appetite.

SINS OF THE HEART: Envy, Jealousy, Enmity, and Rivalry.

Heart sins are dangerous. Have you, like me, ever mistakenly believed that your thoughts are your own business? Or that as long as you do not say it out loud, it is OK to think it? Or that thoughts only become sin if you act on them? Paul includes heart sins as works of the flesh, corrupting seed. Essentially, this moves sin outside the confines of "breaking law," and into the recesses of the human heart.

Self-Check: How is your heart? Many "visitors" present themselves daily at the gates of your heart, calling out to you for entrance and reception. It is up to you which call is answered, and which is ignored.

When "that person" in your life receives accolades and honor, though she worked half as hard and half as long as you, envy may arise. Will you invite it inside for a feast of personal injustice? Or let it pass by unheeded, as you enumerate God's blessings upon your life?

When "that family member" drives you to tour her better-than-yours house, in a better-than-yours car, despite decades of worse-than-yours attitudes, and worse-than-yours spirituality, jealousy may seek a place in you. Will you welcome it as a justifiable ally? Or turn your back on it, setting your mind on the beauty of a relationship with the God of all creation?

When someone delivers a report of how "those people" across town scorn, condescend and belittle you *(again)*, cast shade on your motives *(again)*, call into question your efforts *(again)*, enmity may flare up brightly at your gate. Will you fan and fuel the flames with outrage as you review the unprovoked, unjustified history of their scoffing? Or quell the threatening flame with the overflowing, God-supplied, living water of peace and kindness?

When "that uninvited acquaintance" gears up for another self-constructed competition as reassurance against her inadequacies, rivalry may desire to show her up. Will you engage in the meaningless battle for superiority? Or give way to her, esteeming her as better than yourself, realizing her core need for acceptance?

Heart sins threaten at the level of thoughts and intents. For every woman of faith, the Living Word of God reigns over even these least acknowledged alcoves of the heart *(Heb. 4:12)*. As the visitors of envy, jealousy, enmity, and rivalry call out for attention, God empowers us to turn away as we call out to Him in times of temptation. We all understand the resulting alternative of ugliness, rot, and sin when such ungodly visitors live unchallenged within us.

SINS OF THE MOUTH: Strife, Dissensions, Divisions, and Outbursts of Wrath

Mouth sins are destructive. The Mosaic Law primarily regulated rites, regulations, and ceremonies, but rarely addressed the importance of upright speech. Paul's inclusion of deleterious words as manifestations of flesh-seed corruption moves the conception of sin away from "law-breaking," and into accountability for the use of language.

Not surprisingly, the mouth sins of strife, dissension, divisions, and outbursts of wrath externally exhibit the internal heart conditions of envy, jealousy, enmity, and rivalry. When sinful thoughts and intents visit, an unwise heart welcomes them, feeds them, and offers them residence. Yet, the Creator of human hearts fashioned our hearts as giving vessels—they are designed to pour out contents in service to others. So, when sin rather than the Savior resides inside, loathsome content pour forth. Words thus employed wound, isolate, divide, and segregate. Have you noticed any wounded, isolated, divided, segregated tendencies in the world? How about in your world?

Women of faith know better: we have not so learned Christ *(Eph. 4:20)*. Yet, among the works of the flesh, these represent our most common failing. Why? Because we did not turn these sins away at the thought level, and so they grew. They are common because we are deceived about the profound sinfulness of strife, dissension, and division. They are common because we believe outbursts of wrath are justified by "holy" strife, dissension, and division.

In a masterful twist of deception, Satan, the adversary, often successfully convinces even the *adelphoi*, brothers and sisters within

Christ's body, to use tools of discord, dissension, and division. We make up one interwoven body. We share in one holy blood. Yet, so often, we wound and isolate with sinful words: "If you bite and devour one another, beware lest you be consumed by one another!" *(Gal. 5:15)*.

Yet, there is more. If a woman of faith is deceived about these sins, how can she find her way out? Specifically, what if it is you? What if it is me? Jesus offers the infallible test: "You shall know them by their fruits" *(Matt. 7:16)*. Answer the following questions: What fruit emerges around me? What fruit results from the way I use words? As I honestly assess the abiding and repeating patterns of my life, what do I see?

Employing words according to the adversary's deceitful twisting produces lives marked by strife, dissension, division, and wrath. It produces wounded family members, isolated and divided by pain and distrust. It produces increasing individual isolation, as one's own judgments and sinful word choices break instead of build. It produces

a life populated by one broken relationship after another. Honest personal assessment shines the light of Christ's judgment over our choices.

Jesus offers us a better way. The way of Jesus upholds and maintains truth, without letting go of mercy. Using His revealed interactions as our template saves us from the adversary's deceptive presentation of strife as a tool for holiness. A woman's fits, wrath, and dissension still do "not produce the righteousness of God" *(Jas. 1:20)*.

SINS OF THE BODY: Drunkenness and Orgies (Carousing)

"Drunkenness and carousing" is debauchery. The cultural heritage of Gentiles in Gaul included unrestricted acceptance of occasional, excessive drunkenness, and the associated behaviors of orgies and public debauchery. Paul includes their longstanding, ancient traditions in his condemnation of the flesh-seed mindset.

So many of us enjoy the tremendous advantage of believing parents or grandparents who shared the Word and Way of God with us from the earliest moments of life. Drunkenness, debauchery, and orgies exist distantly outside even the outermost protective boundaries of God's reign in us. Godly women respond to such by saying, "We would never!" It should be so, but our sober lifestyle does not extend to the myriad millions. In an article entitled, "Who Gets Drunk More Often Than Americans?", Jack Guy reports that a 2019 survey in thirty countries found a world-wide average of thirty-three days per year of excessive drunkenness. English-speaking countries averaged much higher:

Country	Average Drunk Days per Year
United Kingdom	51
United States	50
Canada	48
Australia	47
World-wide	33

These numbers represent people you know. One out of four people in your acquaintance *(but hopefully not Christians)* participates in at least one monthly drinking binge. Extrapolating the chart above to the lives of average Americans in your neighborhood indicates a full-on drunken episode every 7.3 days—once a week! For many, alcohol is not enough, and cocaine represents a cleaner, quicker, easily accessible alternative. Delivery of a cocaine stash takes about as long as the delivery of a pizza: thirty minutes. For some, cocaine seems too expensive, and marijuana is a *(sometimes)* legal, and *(somewhat)* cost-effective alternative.

Debauchery follows close behind alcohol and drugs. As those who rest safely within the peace and privilege of fellowship with God, these behaviors baffle. Why? Why do they choose these things?

Women of faith respond by asking, "Why on earth? Why do they choose alcohol? Why do they move on to cocaine? Why do they get stoned and act ridiculous? Why do they sell their souls in carousing and lust?" I believe the answer is simple. I believe they seek what we already possess: deliverance from pain and shame, peace of heart and mind, comfort and joy of belonging, assurance, and confidence of true love. We possess all these surpassing benefits as the redeemed ones, washed in the cleansing blood of Christ. We exist in safety, "hidden with Christ in God" (Col. 3:3).

For those who do not yet know the enduring Word and Way of God, alcohol and marijuana offer oblivion, numbness, and peace. Cocaine supplies elation and joy. Carousing companions offer belonging and fellowship. Lust and sexual pleasures substitute for assurance and faithful love.

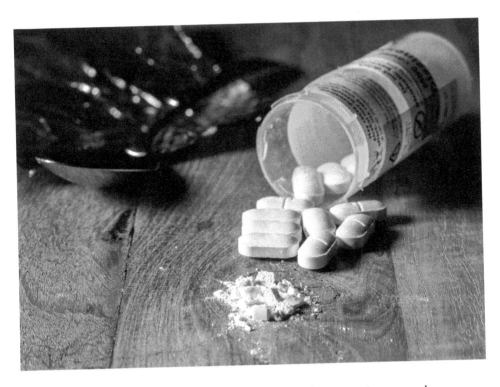

Do you begin to understand their "why"? The emptiness and desperation of life outside of Christ can never excuse sin. However, privileged children of God who approach each lost one's emptiness and desperation with hearts of mercy may lead them to the One who can forgive sin, delivering them from the pain. We all want and need the same things. You and I know the True Source. *Let's tell them about Him, too.*

Conclusion

Flesh deceives. Sadly, the putrefaction of sinful flesh inhabited the region of Galatia, threatening newly redeemed Christians who dwelt there. How could it threaten their faith? As we learned, the same works of flesh inhabit our region today. We share the same danger the Galatians experienced. Decay and stench are obvious. The ruin of sin is obvious. Surely the brothers and sisters, beloved *adelphoi*, in Galatia would never choose stench, rot, and ruin over Jesus Christ! Surely they would never greedily feed their own flesh appetites, oblivious to the smell and decay! Yet, some among them did; and some among us do, too. Why? Because the flesh deceives.

Dear woman of faith, do you want to inherit the kingdom of God *(Gal. 5:21)*? I know you do. Do you want your life to bring forth that beautiful fruit, born of Spirit-seed *(5:22-23)*? I know you do. Do you want to walk by God's Spirit, be led by God's Spirit, and live by God's Spirit *(5:16, 18, 25)*? I know you do. I encourage you to "crucify the flesh with its passions and desires."

If any of these works of flesh entangle you, perhaps you have already thought of this. You already know that you want to put off such works! So what can you do? Pray hard, and try your best. If you succeed, praise God. If you fail, get up and pray again, then try again. And again. And again. As many times as it takes to overcome. "The one who overcomes shall inherit all things, and I will be *(her)* God, and *(she)* will be my child" *(Rev. 21:7)*. It is absolutely worth it. Christ is worth it all.

Thought Questions

1. From your reading of Galatians, why do you think returning to "circumcision" was such a big deal?

2. Is it necessary for a woman of faith to actively filter the music, television, movies, fiction, etc. that she regularly consumes? If so, why? If not, why not?

   Please provide at least two Scriptural references to uphold your answer.

3. In your circle, are there any people who struggle with sexual immorality or sensuality? How does this sin affect their lives? How does this sin affect others?

4. In current American pop culture, what do you notice about the resurrection of idolatrous thought?

5. Do you see any comparisons between popular superheroes and ancient gods/ goddesses?

6. Can you think of any TV shows, movies, or books that seem to popularize witchcraft or sorcery?

7. Is there any aspect of idolatrous belief or practice that appeals to you? Or to your children? Explain the appeal and find Scriptures that address those ideas.

8. Why do you think heart and mouth sins feel "safer" to Christians than other works of the flesh?

9. How is it possible for a woman of faith to actively halt and remove the seeds of heart and mouth sins in her daily walk?

10. Are there any people in your acquaintance who participate in drunkenness, drugs, and carousing? Why is it hard to see past their sin? How can you align your heart to desire to reach out to them (not just faking it, or because it is "the right thing") with the good news about Jesus?

11. What do you think is the best approach to leading someone away from the pull of the works of the flesh?

Concept Seeds

To begin preparation for the next lesson, please consider the following question: Is the condition of a person's heart soil static or ever-changing? Are there any verses that helped you with your answer?

Soil in Galatia

Lesson 5: Introduction

It was another one of those ambitious super-mom schemes. Fourteen years ago, I ordered five pounds of "organic, non-GMO winter wheat berries" *(i.e., wheat seeds)*. That season's pioneering plan involved soaking, sprouting, smashing, and baking those berries into "homemade sprouted organic, non-GMO wheatberry bread" for family nourishment. I completed the process exactly once. After Homer the Dog refused the resulting dense, soggy mush, I threw the remaining four pounds of wheat berries into the deep freezer where they rested peacefully for the next eleven years.

Seeds need soil. Eventually, we bought a farm and knew just what to do. Resurrecting the long-frozen wheat berries, we entrusted them to my husband's new farming "skills" for planting. Wow! What an abundant harvest resulted! Even after years of apparent dormancy, those seeds internally maintained indefatigable life-force and potential. Under the sun's warm light, by the trickling country creek, planted in soil that had been properly prepared, vigorous energy ignited into wheat life. "He who supplies seed to the sower and bread for food will supply and multiply your seed for sowing and increase the harvest of your righteousness. You will be enriched in every way to be generous in every way, which through us will produce thanksgiving to God" *(2 Cor. 9:10-11)*. Sowing activates the seeds' densely compacted internal potential. Seeds need soil.

Heart Soil

Your heart is soil. In Christ, "you are God's field" *(1 Cor. 3:9)*. You are the field, or territory, belonging to God. The kingdom of heaven expands in you and through you—wielding transformative power and influence. Jesus explained, "The kingdom of God does not come with observation.

Nor will they say, 'Look, here it is!' or 'There!' For behold, the kingdom of God is within you" *(Luke 17:20)*. We all believe these words of Jesus, but may still wonder how? How does the kingdom of heaven find its way into your heart? It arrives at your heart's gate, as it does in every other heart who hears the word. It arrives as potential. It arrives as seed *(Matt. 13:24)*. Woman of faith, *you* are God's field.

In first-century Galatia, as in twenty-first-century America, the hearts of men and women comprised the field and vineyard of God. Through Paul, the sower, the gospel seed, alive with potential to save and transform, arrived in Galatia. "The word of God *is* living and powerful" *(Heb. 4:12)*, triggering immediate reactions and changes when sown in the hearts of humanity. "So shall My word be that goes forth from My mouth; It shall not return to Me void, but it shall accomplish what I please, And it shall prosper in the thing for which I sent it" *(Isa. 55:11)*. In first-century Galatia, dramatic reforms initiated as the seed, God's living and powerful word, encountered the soil of human hearts. Are you meekly accepting the alterations wrought by God's word within you? As C.S. Lewis once wrote:

> *Imagine yourself as a living house. God comes in to rebuild that house. At first, perhaps, you can understand what He is doing. He is getting the drains right and stopping the leaks in the roof and so on: you knew that those jobs needed doing and so you are not surprised. But presently he starts knocking the house about in a way that hurts abominably and does not seem to make sense. What on earth is He up to? The explanation is that He is building quite a different house from the one you thought of—throwing out a new wing here, putting on an extra floor there, running up towers, making courtyards. You thought you were going to be made into a decent little cottage: but He is building a palace. He intends to come and live in it Himself* (Mere Christianity, 205).

Good Soil in Galatia

Good soil, receiving the pure gospel of God, brings forth fruit—"some a hundredfold, some sixty, and some thirty" *(Matt. 13:23)*. Paul entered Galatia as a good-soil heart, scattering the seed of the kingdom. Many

hearts in Galatia received that gospel and bore fruit, so much so that by the time Paul penned his letter to them, he addressed it to several "churches" in Galatia *(Gal. 1:2)*. What kind of hearts made up those "churches"?

Good-Soil Hearts?

This letter to our brothers and sisters in Galatia illuminates, as an essential core concept, that every one of us lives either by spirit or flesh. Two options exist, and we must choose one or the other. Opting for part of one and part of the other cannot work. "For the desires of the flesh are against the Spirit, and the desires of the Spirit and against the flesh, for these are opposed to each other" *(Gal. 5:17)*. We must choose all of one or all of the other.

Because He is God, "Spirit" gifted humanity with the word-revealing, teaching, and offering great and precious promises. Through the word, God's Spirit proclaims God's invitation to faith *(Rom. 10:17)*, and His offer of life *(Rom. 8:10)*. Through His chosen apostles and prophets, the Holy Spirit reveals the age-spanning mystery and plan of God to bring us into a relationship with Him *(Eph. 3:5)*. The Spirit did not just present some themes to them, hoping that imperfect men could find the right words to reveal His perfect will. The Spirit taught them exactly which words to use, in order to best enable our understanding of the mind of Christ *(1 Cor. 2:7-16)*. Accordingly, all Scripture is inspired by God *(2 Tim. 3:16)*. The Spirit's perfect, preserved words offer enduring illumination of God's purpose, so that even today, you and I can read and understand *(Eph. 3:4)*. Through His time-traversing invitation, "Come out from among them and be separate" *(2 Cor. 6:17)*, the Spirit invites you and me into a shared spiritual life. This is living "by the Spirit," which aligns with Christ. In Paul, as well as other Galatians who proved fruitful, good-soil hearts received the implanted Word. Good-soil hearts then and now live "by the Spirit" *(Gal. 5:25)*.

So What Happened?

There was corruption in Galatia. Paul said, "I am astonished that you are so quickly deserting him who called you in the grace of Christ and are turning to a different gospel" *(Gal. 1:6)*. He was shocked, astonished, or, as my daughter might say, "shook." He expected better from them. He expected good from them. He expected faithfulness from them.

Have you ever felt this way as pressures of the faith-walk inevitably reveal residual character deficits in those whom you love and respect? Have you ever just wanted to grab someone by the shoulders, demanding, "What on earth are you doing?" Just like us, Paul marveled at the seemingly inexplicable behavior in his fellow Christians. Just like us, he sought understanding.

Thankfully, Christ's perceptive parable about the sower unveils the intrinsic composition of three unfruitful heart-soils. With this clarifying viewpoint, astonishment gives way to awareness: An enemy walks among us. The enemy relentlessly interferes with the seed that Jesus sows, turning hearts aside to a different gospel.

Could It Be Me?

Don't you wish the field of every heart disclosed good-soil characteristics? Perhaps at first, most do. Then the seed goes to work. As that living, active, sharp, piercing word challenges, things become uncomfortable. Depending on their heart soil's composition, people may wrestle the word rather than submitting to it. As a result, troublers develop, bewitching, and distorting, as they cling stubbornly to pre-conversion identity. Under such influence, potentially good-soil hearts manifest wayside, rocky, and thorny compositions. "It is impossible that no offenses should come, but woe to one through whom they come" *(Luke 17:1)*.

Do women of faith ever trouble the body of Christ? As you well know, even beloved sisters within the church may bewitch and distort, often unaware of the emergent effects. The centuries contain the devastation of once-faithful hearts, wrecked by bewitched troublers. All of us recognize this reality—especially as we witness it in other people. However, our call is not to simply acknowledge and emphasize all the mistakes of *other* people. These are easy to see and easy to point out. Nevertheless, God calls women of faith to depths profoundly more piercing than that. God calls us to honestly assess the reality of our own heart's conditions and actions. Have you, like me, ever experienced moments when self superseded others? Or flesh won instead of spirit? Moments when indignation "justified" gossip? Or the need to be heard rationalized exaggeration? The residue of those dark moments generates an aching sadness and a hollow pain. This reminds me of Jesus, who died to save me and teach me a better way *(Rom. 5:8-9)*.

He Carried My Sorrows
By Glenda Schales

He carried my sorrows, He bore my griefs,
Was pierced for transgressions, afflicted for peace.
He suffered in anguish, He writhed in pain,
Was smitten, forsaken, abandoned and slain.
Despised and rejected, He knew no sin,
Was crushed for His people, no violence within.
My heart mourns His chast'ning, My tears still fall,
My sin is the reason He gave me His all.
He knew by His stripes I am healed, thru His blood I can kneel,
For by His oppression,
I worship my King.

Because of Christ, every woman of faith leaves past mistakes in the past *(Phil. 3:13)*. In Christ, every woman of faith experiences the joy of forgiveness now *(Isa. 43:25)*. By Christ, every woman of faith rejoices in the hope of a wiser future. Through following Christ, committed hearts discover a better way *(John 14:6)*.

Tragically, evil workers in Galatia were actually "Christians." In His parable, Jesus lays the blame for such gospel gatecrashing at Satan's feet *(Mark 11:14; Luke 8:12)*. This is potentially confusing. How could Christians become evil workers? How could Christ-like converts help Satan? *Diabolos*, our accuser, perseveringly strives to overturn all allegiance to God, expertly infiltrating newly conquered heart soil *(Eph. 6:11)*. Does Satan, the adversary, still possess power and skill to bewitch? Thankfully, God grants time and repentance, enabling His people to "escape the snare of the devil, after being captured by him to do his will" *(2 Tim. 2:25-26)*.

Yes, offenses must come. Seemingly good-soil hearts reveal waysides, rocks, and thorns. Thus, Jesus entreats, "Take heed to yourselves!" *(Luke 17:3)*, because "woe to the one" through whom the offenses come *(Luke 17:1)*. I invite your heart to join mine in this prayer: "Please, Lord, don't let it be me who troubles."

Wayside Soil in Galatia

Wayside soil lies untended, packed, trodden, and easily accessible to birds. When a sower indiscriminately casts seed on the ground, some invariably end up along the barren wayside. In Galatia, Paul sowed the incorruptible Seed of Christ. Living, active seed, full of compact, *dunamis* power *(Rom. 1:16)*, sought a place, even in wayside hearts. Under such conditions *(i.e., the wayside)*, those Galatian hearts did not *(and perhaps could not)* yet understand many things.

Misunderstanding the nature and purpose of freedom in Christ created spiritual desolation, so that evil workers quickly devoured and replaced God's authentic seed with a *(slightly)* different gospel. According to Jesus, this interference by evil workers occurs by the purposeful intent of Satan: "The evil one comes and snatches" the seed *(Matt. 13:19)*; "Satan immediately comes and takes away the Word" *(Mark 4:15)*, and "the devil comes and takes away" *(Luke 8:12)*. There was wayside soil in Galatia.

Rocky Soil in Galatia

Rocky soil is rocky, even in the face of tedious, painstaking efforts to clear the field. On our farm, we discovered an area like this. Before we disturbed the soil by plowing and tilling, this field displayed perfect pastoral beauty—plush green grass, no visible weeds, not a rock in sight. Then we tilled the soil. For weeks and weeks, our three boys enjoyed the addition of "field rock removal" on their daily chore charts.

The instructions were simple: *(1)* Take your five-gallon bucket; *(2)* Fill it with rocks until you can barely carry it; *(3)* Haul it up the driveway; *(4)* Dump it on the rock pile; *(5)* Repeat; *(6)* No complaining.

Is It Raining Rocks?

Over and over, they obediently filled, hauled, and dumped, creating quite an enormous pile of field rocks. Yet every day, more rocks littered the surface of the field! How does that even happen? Does the earth miraculously manifest rocks? Do the clouds nocturnally rain rocks? Does an enemy purposefully re-scatter rocks while we sleep? Thankfully, all is not lost. It turns out that mineral-rich rocks supply much-needed nutrients to the soil. Next for the daily chore charts is the directive for "field rock crushing" and "mineral powder spreading." Rocky soil is rocky, but repurposing offers hope.

So what does that look like in a human heart? Jesus explains, "the one who hears the word and receives it with joy, yet he has no root in himself, endures for a little while. Then when tribulation or persecution arises on account of the word *(the seed)*, immediately he falls away" *(Matt. 13:20-21)*. Like our field's illusory cohesion, this kind of heart soil often displays serene, spiritual solidarity—clear dependence on God, observable good works, with not a sin in sight. Then persecution intensifies, forcing a manifestation of what lies beneath the surface. In Galatia, rocky-soil hearts preferred to please men rather than suffer persecution. They desired to "make a good showing in the flesh. . .only that they may not suffer persecution for the cross of Christ" *(Gal. 6:12)*. Human hearts may contain hidden rocks.

Even Pillars

Soberly, the Scriptures reveal that disruptive persecution may unearth rocks and debris even in loyal pillars like Peter *(Gal. 2:11-14)*, or dedicated encouragers like Barnabas: "Even Barnabas was carried away by their hypocrisy" *(2:13)*. Beloved pillars of strength may draw back in fear, succumbing hypocritically to pressures to conform. Strong leaders may "wither away when the heat comes" *(Matt. 13:6)*. Peter's influence led "the rest of the Jews" to do the same. Barnabas played the hypocrite, which is especially surprising, considering his early defense of Paul. We all have moments of failure. However, unless we continue in hypocrisy, those mistakes need not define our walk. So how can women of faith tell the difference between who is true and who is false? How can we know who to trust? Jesus offers a foolproof test: "You shall know them by their fruits" *(Matt. 7:16)*. Thankfully, repentance is available to all, and God can repurpose even the rocky soil *(Rom. 8:28)*. There was rocky soil in Galatia.

Thorny Soil in Galatia

Thorny soil is thorny. Have you ever experienced the annoyance and agony of warring your way through a thorny thicket? Or felt the sharp slash of betrayal as an unnoticed thorn vine tears your leg while hiking? On our farm, a hilltop view captures the essence of country living in Tennessee. Overlooking a wide valley, dotted with farmhouses, cattle, a meandering creek, and a delightfully ramshackle, red barn, this view defines our property. There is only one problem. Entangled thorns completely cover this particular hillside: thorn bushes, thorn branches, and thorn trees *(Yes, trees—thorn trees are an actual thing.)* Sadly, when we mow the field, everything underneath appears dead and discolored, because the thorns relentlessly extract soil nutrients, never replenishing. Blocking all light, and consuming all moisture, thorns coil and parasitically attach to healthy growth, depriving it until it dies.

In order to reclaim our hilltop, a few steps are necessary: *(1)* Cut all growth down to ground level; *(2)* Dig up each root system, or till the entire field to uproot all existing growth; *(3)* Gather every thorny plant and root into a single pile; *(4)* Burn the resulting pile until it is wholly consumed; *(5)* Burn the entire field surface; *(6)* Re-till the field; *(7)* Burn it again; *(8)* Finally, be vigilant for at least seven years, uprooting any new thorn growth and burning as necessary. Needless to say, burning has become a favored pastime. Thorny soil is thorny.

Jesus untangles this concept, identifying "the worry of the world and the deceitfulness of riches" as thorns that choke the growth of the word *(Matt. 13:22)*. Thorny soil in Galatia manifested in respected Jewish rulers and leaders. Their faith, born of pure gospel seed, choked when losses of this world's treasures of wealth, power, and prestige proved too much. Under pressure, they backtracked, purposefully excluding dissenters: "They make much of you, but for no good purpose. They want to shut you out" *(Gal. 4:17)*. In prideful boasting, they accumulate followers: "For even they themselves do not keep the law, but they desire to have you *(keep the law)*. . .that they may boast in your flesh" *(Gal. 6:13)*. Even among those in positions of leadership, worldly approaches, and the deceitfulness of riches choke the new growth, rendering it ultimately unfruitful *(Matt. 13:22)*. There was thorny soil in Galatia.

Conclusion

Seeds thrive in good soil. Exponentially more than my long-frozen wheat berries, God's incorruptible seed contains inexhaustible *dunamis*—power and potential *(Rom. 1:16)*. This knowledge offers hope to every less-than-perfect, often-failing, always-trying-again woman of faith. What if trials of life, persecutions, or honest self-assessments reveal rocks within your heart soil? What if thorny riches and cares of life in an affluent, competitive society parasitically attach, draining energy and resources—so you begin to choke? Even after years of apparent dormancy, the vibrant seed of God rests undefeated. Find the warm light. Seek the living water. Prepare once again the soil of your heart. Then watch as God's Seed re-ignites within you. Sowing activates the seeds' densely compacted internal capacity. Seeds thrive in good soil

Thought Questions

1. In what way did Jesus encounter "wayside" pressure to compromise the purity of His mission?

2. In what way did Jesus encounter "rocky" pressure from persecution and hypocrisy?

3. In what way did Jesus encounter "thorny" pressure from loss of position, power, or prestige?

4. Without a doubt, Jesus's heart is good soil. What examples from His life demonstrate the goodness and purity of His heart?

5. In Galatia, what external evidence revealed wayside hearts?

6. In Galatia, what external evidence revealed rocky hearts?

7. In Galatia, what external evidence revealed thorny hearts?

8. In Galatia, what temptation led even the pillars into sin?

9. What external evidence reveals wayside, rocky, and thorny hearts in those you know?

10. What, if anything, can be done to convert the three unproductive heart-soils into good-soil hearts?

Concept Seeds

To begin preparation for the next lesson, please consider the following question:

How do you feel when you reflect upon God's gifts and provision in your life? Can you find any verses in the Psalms that help express your feelings?

Fruit in Galatia

Lesson 6: Introduction

In the end, a lizard enlightened me. While vacationing last week, my youngest daughter caught a few lizards—specifically, she caught chameleons. We enjoyed quite a show of shifting colors, as the skin of each altered, blending with various backgrounds. Brown on the tree, green on the leaves, light brown on the children's hands, and *(hysterically)* even grey to match my husband's hair! As I patiently endured reptiles, I realized the mistake of these Judaizing teachers. By continuing to bind parts of the law, they reduced their Christianity to an external "change of color." Before learning about Christ, their identity rooted itself in adherence to Moses's law. After confessing allegiance to Christ and being baptized in His name, their identity still anchored in dedication to the covenant of Sinai. Their "color"

changed, but the change was only skin-deep—just like my daughter's chameleons.

A New Creature

A new creature is completely new. God does not call us to color-shift like a chameleon. He calls us to intentional death and crucifixion of all that defined our walk before Christ. He calls us to revolutionary rebirth from the inside out. To the Galatians, Paul emphasized that once a person was in Christ, "neither circumcision avails anything, nor uncircumcision, but a new creature" *(Gal. 6:15)*. This term, creature *(ktisis)*, denotes an original formation by the act of a Creator.

Do you want to be in Christ, completely new? Every Christian is buried with Christ in baptism, putting off the body of the sins of the flesh *(Col. 2:11)*. Every Christian is baptized, putting on Christ *(Gal. 3:27)*. Every Christian is raised with Christ through faith in the working of God. Paul explains this process as the "circumcision not made with hands," or "the circumcision of Christ" *(Col. 2:11)*. In an authentic way, each person of faith is born again *(John 3:3)*. This birth of water and Spirit results in one becoming a new creature *(2 Cor. 5:17)*. One's old flesh identity is cut off, as Christ is put on *(Col. 2:11)*. Have you put on Christ *(Gal. 3:27)*? If so, you are completely new, no longer identified by flesh standards. Your change reaches far beyond a skin-deep color-shift. Transformed by God, a new creature is entirely new.

Copy Jesus

So what are you now that you are in Christ? You are the Spirit's fruit. In obedience to the implanted Word, the seed of God, women of faith conform their will, words, and deeds to the image of Christ *(Rom. 8:29)*. The Spirit's fruit copies Jesus. During His sojourn among us, humanity experienced Christ's light, as He externally manifested the invisible attributes of the Father: "He is the image of the invisible God" *(Col. 1:15)*. Our task is to copy Jesus, being "imitators of God, as beloved children" *(Eph. 5:1)*, manifesting the invisible worth and excellence of God. Is this the way you think of your Christianity? Do you recognize that your faith leads you to imitate Jesus? Do you understand that your work is

to live out your recognition of deity? Does your faith lead you to draw attention to God's goodness through your actions? God sent Jesus, His Seed, to demonstrate by visible activity the invisible nature of God. As new creatures in Christ's body, He calls us to do the same.

Love

By Jesus's actions, we comprehend that God is love *(1 John 4:8)*. The gospel accounts attest to the many facets of His love. Ultimately, His greatest exhibition of love resulted in a complete sacrifice of self and self-will for our good: "Walk in love, just as Christ also loved you and gave Himself up" *(Eph. 5:2)*.

Joy

By Jesus's actions, we glimpse that God is joy and radiates joy. Through steadfast obedience, Jesus abode in His father's love. By so doing, He experienced undefeatable joy. If we continue in His words, the gift of joy is born within us as well: "These things I have spoken to you so that My joy may be in you" *(John 15:11)*.

Peace

By Jesus's actions, we witness that God is peace and confers peace. "Peace I leave with you; My peace I give to you" *(John 14:27)*. As seasoned fishermen trembled in the storm, Jesus commanded, "Peace be still" *(Mark 4:39)*. Later, He showed confident peace in His Father's will, just hours before his arrest, stating, "These things I have spoken to you, that in Me you may have peace. In the world, you will have tribulation; but be of good cheer, I have overcome the world" *(John 16:33)*.

Patience

By Jesus's actions, we perceive that God is patient and establishes patience. The patience of the Scriptures and long-suffering of God culminated in the birth of the Spirit's seed through the body of the virgin Mary, "for nothing will be impossible with God" *(Luke 1:37)*. In the same way, Jesus patiently endured, leaving us an example to follow *(1 Pet. 2:21)*. Rather than enduring a life in which our snared souls mindlessly serve sin, patience assures us that we, too, can "possess our souls" *(Luke 21:19)*.

Kindness

By Jesus's actions, we recognize that God is kind and practices kindness. The kindness of Jesus unfailingly answers, "I am willing" *(Matt. 8:3)*, "I will come," and "I will heal" *(Matt. 8:7)*, even to untouchable lepers, unclean women *(Luke 8:48)*, and unworthy sinners *(Mark 2:15-17)*. He calls us to do the same: "Be kind to one another, tenderhearted, forgiving one another" *(Eph. 4:32)*.

Goodness

By Jesus's actions, we observe that God is good and defines goodness. Followers of Jesus recognized the perpetual goodness of both the words and deeds of Jesus, addressing Him as "Good Teacher" *(Luke 18:18-20)*. Unwittingly, with this label of respect, men identified the truth of His deity, because only One is truly good *(Luke 18:19)*. Because we are born of Him, He likewise calls us to "do good to all" *(Gal. 6:10)*.

Faithfulness

By Jesus's actions, we experience that God is faithful and performs faithfully. The presence and faithfulness of Jesus never disappoint. To the young children who sought His blessing, Jesus was faithful. To the widow who lost her son, Jesus was faithful. To Jarius, the lepers, the blind, the demon-possessed, He was faithful. To the will of God for His own death, Jesus was faithful. Therefore, His faithful sacrifice of blood ensures God's promise, "If we confess our sins, He is faithful and just to forgive us our sins and cleanse us from all unrighteousness" *(1 John 1:9)*.

Gentleness

By Jesus's actions, we perceive that God is gentle and exhibits gentleness. He invites us into the demonstration of meekness, born of a gentle heart. "Take my yoke upon you and learn from me, for I am meek and lowly in heart" *(Matt. 11:29)*.

Self-Control

By Jesus's actions, we discern that God is self-controlled and models self-control. Submitted to the will of His Father, Jesus committed Himself to purposeful fulfillment of His role, refusing to exercise His own free-will subversively. "Or do you think that I cannot appeal to My Father, and He will at once put at My disposal more than twelve legions of angels? But how then will the Scriptures be fulfilled, which say that it must happen this way?" *(Matt. 26:53-54)*. In the same way, women of faith welcome the reign of Christ within us but steadfastly resist sin's desire to reign in our mortal bodies *(Rom. 6:12-14)*.

Our Lord's actions transformed deity's invisible characteristics into forms tangible to the flesh. This is no longer a mystery. The invisible God manifested His invisible divine attributes to humanity through the life of

Jesus. While on earth, Jesus demonstrated externally every facet of the Spirit's fruit. Now that we belong to Him, He calls us to follow His steps. The Spirit's fruit is copying Jesus.

Copying Jesus in Galatia

In Galatia, "many disciples" *(Acts 14:21; 18:23)* put on Christ, composing several local congregations *(Acts 14:23; 16:4-6)*. Even though they increased in number daily, the New Testament record reveals almost no names of Christians from that region. Further, both Scriptural and historical records render it nearly impossible to determine the exact boundaries and locations known as "Galatia." No known names. No definite sense of place. No "reputation" among the brotherhood. Christians in the "mainstream" *(at that time, Jerusalem and Antioch of Syria)* barely knew they existed. Yet, God knew those who were His and where they dwelt *(2 Tim. 2:19)*.

Two "Southern" Women

Despite all the mystery and ambiguity from this region, God highly honors two Galatian women from the middle of nowhere. People in Lystra talked differently than most Romans, generally in their local dialect, rather than the universal Greek language *(Acts 14:11)*. Although Amyntas, king of Galatia, deeded the town over to emperor Augustus in 36 BC, the famous Roman roads never made it out to their native region until after Jesus was born. Even when a road was finally constructed in AD 6, Lystra was the end of the line. In fact, the district, "Lycaonia," or "wolf land," barely earned inclusion on the maps. Yet, in the midst of "wolf land," God noticed the quiet faith of two women, recording their names, detailing their results, trumpeting their influence through young Timothy, who was converted to Christ under their careful tutelage. Two of God's Galatian lambs faithfully flourished in the middle of "wolf land." Lois and Eunice, whose example has profoundly affected women of faith throughout the ages, dwelt in a backwater town in southern Galatia.

When Paul the sower first traveled through southern Galatia *(Acts 14:6-7)*, Lois and Eunice heard the gospel about Jesus, Son of God, and believed *(Acts 16:1-2)*. With them, young Timothy was near as angry men rejected Jesus and tried to kill Paul, the sower, by casting stones at him until he lay in the street, seemingly dead *(Acts 14:19-20)*. Understanding the turmoil associated with their first encounter with the gospel of Christ, we recognize that women of faith learn. Walking by faith is not only for the quiet, peaceful seasons of life. Notably, a walk of faith rises in those moments, days, and years that test, try, and threaten our conviction.

Does Any of this Matter?

I wonder, did Lois or Eunice ever falter, as odds stacked against their determined intention to reflect Christ and equip young Timothy with God's gospel seed? There, in Galatia, heroes displayed hypocrisy. Some of the leading men created conflict and division. Satan waged violent war against the church. Do you think their daily burden in the yoke of Christ ever felt heavy? Of course! Lois and Eunice felt just as you or I often feel: "Your family of believers all over the world is going through the same kind of sufferings" *(1 Pet. 5:9, NLT)*.

We may be tempted to think, "My task feels small. My impact seems nil. My role feels unimportant." Do not believe these lies. In the regions of ancient Galatia and your region today, God purposefully designed a supremely impactful role for women of faith. Does God know what He is doing? Does God understand what is most needful for His kingdom? Does God comprehend the needs of your family? "As for God, His way is perfect; the Lord's word is flawless" (Ps. 18:30, NIV). Our omniscient God wisely concentrates the primary duties of women of faith within the home. Contentedly centered in God's plan, women of faith follow the Spirit-revealed blueprint. Radiating from the home, honorable women diligently produce provision, not only for their own families but also for hired employees, and the forgotten poor. Such abundant supply happens on purpose through business endeavors, duties within community and government spheres, buying and selling of property, and even vineyard planting. Lydia, Dorcas, Deborah, and Mrs. Proverbs 31 all follow this template of capable industry. Whether single, married, mother, aunt, grandmother, teacher, sister, friend—God designates the care and sphere of home life to women of faith (Titus 2:3-5).

Recently, a well-meaning Christian counseled my 19-year-old daughter: "I hope you are not settling for life, doing nothing more than being at home. You have so much to offer! With your talents, you need to find your place. You can change the world! Don't throw all that away being a housewife!" Have you ever heard, or perhaps felt, such sentiments yourself? Even among faithful Christians, God's plan often feels counterintuitive considering our cultural immersion in an opposing mindset. In the church, intelligent, capable women often feel propelled out of the home as they seek ways to steward their God-given talents. Leaving home and family duties to someone else is an inviting path, especially as seemingly simple or mundane duties of homemaking chip away at dignity. Among women of faith who initially choose to concentrate talents within the God-ordained sphere of the home, relentless daily demands present a reoccurring challenge.

Every single day is an endless loop of cook, feed, clean, then repeat—Every. Single. Day. When "Mount Washmore" spills out of the laundry room, and people trip on it; when every meal smacks of burned toast; when your brain turns to mush because you spend every shred of

intelligence on the fine-tuned organization of various concoctions of slime versus play dough. . .the threat of burnout is real. Then, as the husband breezes in from work at 6:00 p.m., it's time to plaster on the "welcome-home-to-the-perfect-wife-and-family" smile. Have you ever felt this way? If so, you are not alone. You are not a failure just because you may feel overwhelmed. You are not sinning because the realities of home life sometimes rattle your sanity. Dear sister, we are in this together. God's plan often seems counterintuitive.

It Says What It Says

It is OK to feel all these things, but women of faith do not make decisions and build lives on what we feel. We make decisions, and build our lives on what the Lord says. Regarding our role, the inspired apostle Paul instructed:

. . .The older women likewise, that they be reverent in behavior, not slanderers, not given to much wine, teachers of good things—that they admonish the young women to love their husbands, to love their children, to be discreet, chaste, homemakers, good, obedient to their own husbands, that the word of God may not be blasphemed (Titus 2:3-5).

Women of faith turn again to God's revealed and confirmed word. God has the answers we need, just as He provided answers for our sisters, Lois and Eunice, so long ago. When the world feels upside down, we look upward. As centuries of tradition are upended overnight, we maintain. When tensions and tempers run high, even to the level of public violence *(such as occurred with the public stoning of Paul)*, we prayerfully wait. When local church leadership falters and shifts under the influence of troublers, women of faith quietly hold fast to God's clear revelation. Bestowing great honor, God names Lois and Eunice, revealing from their stories key characteristics needed to bring forth spiritual fruit. Through the legacy of our Galatian sisters, God teaches us, if we are willing to learn.

Unfeigned Faith

In stark contrast to local leaders, even pillars, who fell prey to pressures of hypocritical conformity, God described the faith of these women as "unfeigned" *(2 Tim. 1:5)*. They were not play-actors behind hypocritical masks. They were not projecting false images of perfection. They were not fake. Day by day, unfeigned faith patiently poured God's Holy Scriptures into the malleable heart of young Timothy. Raising a son who is a faithful disciple of Jesus, well-reported by the brethren in multiple cities, and chosen companion to Paul, the apostle, all before he is even 20 years old, requires purposeful intention and daily diligence. Despite the surrounding friction about Jesus's message, unfeigned, home-centered faith propelled these Galatian women into more profound commitment and service. Each day, these two women in Galatia awoke, determined to copy Jesus. Unbounded by time, their projection of true faith profoundly reflects the image of Jesus, glorifying God.

Obviously, no woman of faith sets out to feign faith. No woman of faith aspires to be a sham. Yet, it happens. Sometimes unknowingly, it happens. Even well-intentioned Christians commonly settle into destructive patterns of "feigned faith." So, how can we discern the difference between unfeigned faith and the play actor's mask? First, in myself, and then, in others, how can I tell the difference?

Ask yourself, "Who am I copying? Who am I pleasing? Who gets the glory?" Exhibiting "righteous" reactions to injustice, difficulty, and hardship like a badge of emotional martyrdom mimics dramatic womanhood but does not copy Jesus. Playing the game of who's "in" or who's "out" might delight those who like to have the preeminence, but it does not please God. Justifying abandonment of God's revealed patterns to multiply your impact glorifies self, but does not glorify God.

Unfeigned faith is frighteningly real. The deceitful safety of the play actor's mask powerfully pulls. Even so, authentic Christianity resolutely removes the mask, exhibiting quiet, childlike trust in the wisdom of a great God. It is a little like stripping away every carefully constructed guard against hurts, injustices, and betrayals, and opening yourself to even more. Living with "hearts wide open" *(2 Cor. 6:11)*, women of faith fearlessly exhibit unfeigned faith, which pleases God.

Unfailing Service

In stark contrast to local leaders who quickly turned away from the truth of Christ, this mother and grandmother exhibited unfailing service. Pouring themselves out in the hope of God's future blessing, they recognized no immediate fleshly reward. How else would they have trained up young Timothy? As the Holy Spirit underscores, they "nourished" him in the words of faith *(1 Tim. 4:6)*. Every woman understands this idea of nourishing a child. They fed him, pampered him, and fattened him up on the rich *Logos* of God. Nourishing does not happen overnight; rather, it demands an ongoing, around-the-clock outpouring of nutrients and care.

Once home needs are met, women of faith focus on serving the household of God. In what way can a woman of faith today nourish souls within her influence? Galatians 6 offers several opportunities.

Restorer of Souls

It is easy to read, but hard to do: "If anyone is overtaken in a trespass, you who are spiritual restore such a one in the spirit of gentleness" *(Gal. 6:1)*. Have you ever been overtaken, or carried away by a surprise attack of sin? Have you ever failed? If so, how did you feel when you realized your sin? Defeated? Ashamed? Hopeless? How about wanting to hide under the bed in a fetal position and never come out? How about the mocking discouragement that leaves you with no strength to even try? Every woman of faith encounters these depths. Sin wounds deeply, resulting in a profound need for reassurance coupled with accountability. Having faced the defeat of sin themselves, those who are spiritual gently restore others.

Bearer of Burdens

In the first instance, women of genuine faith reach out to bear one another's burdens *(Gal. 6:2)*. The Greek word *baros*, translated "burden," identifies a sinking load; a weight that bows down; the heaviness endured by those who must work without reprieve through the heat of the day. It means to "experience something that is particularly

oppressive" *(BDAG, 167)*. As we witness seasons of such burdens upon others, we want to help. Unlike the Pharisees who bound heavy burdens on others, those who are spiritual seek to fulfill the law of Christ by relieving others in times of trial. Bear one another's burdens.

In the second instance, women of faith bear their own burden *(Gal. 6:5)*. Paul refers to the daily burden of every Christian, which Jesus described: "My burden is light." This daily backpack of personal responsibility comprises activities and endeavors which are best accomplished by you. "Love the Lord your God with all your heart" *(cf. Mark 12:30)* is personal for you. "Love your neighbor as yourself" *(Gal. 5:14)* requires service that only you can provide. "Love your husband" *(cf. Titus 2:4b)* is for you and no one else. "Love your children" *(cf. Titus 2:4c)* calls for you, and no one can replace you. "Keep your home" *(cf. 1 Tim. 5:14)* involves the focused, effective oversight carried out by you. "Teacher of good things" *(cf. Titus 2:3)* requires insights specific to you. Individual tasks within each of these roles may be delegated, but the burden of responsibility rests on you. Bear your own burden.

Doer of Good

As a part of the daily load of personal responsibilities, God calls each of us to "do good" to all, "especially to the household of faith" *(Gal. 6:10)*. However, this is not a mere checklist. This involves bearing fruit. Doing good to all flows naturally from the spiritual heart. Hearts and eyes trained by the Spirit of God focus outward in the same way as Jesus's heart focused outward. The Spirit-filled heart overflows because of God's goodness *(Eph. 5:18)*. There is no lack; no need to hoard kind words or deeds; no need to cling to worldly goods. Sharing and giving proceed naturally.

Unshakeable Foundations

In stark contrast to local leaders led away by "a different gospel," Lois and Eunice held firmly to the once-delivered faith. In dedicated faith, they committed their moments and days to the *Logos* of faith who reveals God's precious words. On this bedrock, they fattened, pampered, and reared Timothy in the rich nourishment of God's good *(beautiful, valuable, virtuous)* **doctrine** *(1 Tim. 4:6)*.

Don't you want to do this for your children, grandchildren, and students? What does this look like on a daily basis? Can I share an approach that I used? I am tremendously blessed with a husband who is committed to the spiritual training of our children. As his helper and fellow heir in the grace of life, I long to be useful and involved, shoring up and supporting him in this eternally consequential task. As a young mother, my heart desired to follow this example of Lois and Eunice. Yet, trial and error revealed that I am not one of those women who can successfully stick to any kind of complicated plan while maintaining sanity. Somehow, by the grace of God, I was able to keep hold of one simple habit: *Center on God.*

As an expectant mother of three small children, I had long ago given up perfect motherhood, and the perfectly executed daily schedule, but was determined to hold tight to God. So each morning, clean paper and markers followed breakfast bowls. The children and I opened God's word together. "What will the Lord teach us today?" Beginning in Genesis, we traveled through the Scriptures in order, pulling out an 8-10 minute reading directly from the Scriptures. The children had a very important duty of illustrating the readings, which sometimes took them another 10 minutes. Each day, we attached the new illustrations around the top of the dining room wall. It was fun to watch it grow. First, a lone picture hung randomly above the dining buffet; then, a few; and, a few more; finally, it went all the way around the room! All summer long, neighborhood visitors, family, and friends curiously questioned: What is happening in this picture? Why are the dinosaurs under the water? Why is that king so fat? Why are the people so sad? Who is this man touching the sick people? Each trip around the wall equated to about one-third of the Bible story. So, after three times around *(over three years)*, we completed Genesis to Revelation! Wow!

Then, we did it again, from Genesis to Revelation—just mom, the kids, and the seed, which is the word of God. For the second trip through the Scriptures, pictures gained detail; then, 1-2 sentence narratives; then, entire paragraphs. We all learned so much! For the first few years, I thought I was teaching the children. Then I realized, God was teaching us all. Nearly fifteen years have passed since the children and I hung that first picture on the wall. Though much has changed, I still have trouble balancing complicated programs and sanity. So for us, almost every school morning begins around the same table—just mom, the kids, and the seed, which is the word of God. Center on God. There is nothing—*not one thing*—in the world more valuable for the souls of your children than the ongoing habit of few quiet moments with the seed of God.

What young souls are within the scope of your influence? I encourage you to follow the example of these two women in southern Galatia. Nourish up the children on the rich *Logos* of God. Feed them on His good doctrine. Pamper them with His love. Like Lois and Eunice, women of faith rise, meeting physical needs, while laying spiritual foundations. By faith, we understand that the "good doctrine" of God powerfully trains the hearts of youth from the inside out *(1 Tim. 4:6)*. Good doctrine is contained in the good seed *(Matt. 13:27)*, which is sown in good soil *(Matt. 13:23)*, producing good fruit *(Matt. 3:10; 7:17)*, which involves doing good *(Gal. 6:9)*. By patient endurance, Lois and Eunice bore the Spirit's fruit in Galatia. In your place, you can do the same today.

Faith or Works?

So, let's take this a little deeper. As earnest students of Paul's letter to the Galatians, let's challenge ourselves. What should we emulate from the lives of Lois and Eunice? Their faith, or their works? Which made the difference for Timothy? Their unfeigned faith, or their unselfish works? It is not an easy question. As you consider your answer, I offer you some thoughts for reflection.

Seeking Justification by Faith or Justification by Works?

Galatians offers a contrast between Spirit-seed versus flesh-seed, which equates to faith in Christ versus works of law. You and I both know that the apparent tug-of-war between faith and works often feels impossible to understand. For every woman of faith, regardless of background, it is easier to just stick to what we know for sure and ignore teachings that challenge our comfort zone. Because of my upbringing and life experience, working harder makes more sense to me than trusting deeper and abiding closer. For me, it is easier to confidently

defend God's right to require obedience than to defend His willingness to extend grace. Because of your upbringing and life experience, the opposite may be true.

Yet God revealed the truth of both perspectives. God revealed justification by faith: "Knowing that a man is not justified by works of the law, but by faith in Jesus Christ" *(Gal. 2:16)*; and God revealed justification by works: "You see then that a man is justified by works, and not by faith alone" *(Jas. 2:24)*. Both are true. Because of Galatians, we grasp that the works which justify are those that emerge as the outgrowth of faith. As God demonstrated with Abraham, good works are the fruit, not the root of faith. Apart from faith, religious law-keeping serves flesh, not Spirit. As women of faith, we make our stand at the narrow junction of divine truth, accepting both as completely true, and rejecting neither.

This necessity of accepting both justification by faith *and* justification by works stretches my understanding. How can both be true, when they seem to be mutually exclusive doctrines? This seems impossible. My heart and my mind want to choose one or the other, but I believe the Bible is the approved word of God, and the Bible says both. Lois and Eunice bore the Spirit's fruit, as their *faith worked*, to the glory of God.

Bind Us Together, Lord

We are in Christ now, and in Christ, it is all about "faith working through love" *(Gal. 5:6)*. When faith works through love, that is called fruit. When the seed, which is the word, grows within a heart to such a degree that it motivates external action, that is called fruit. When the divine Word, Jesus Christ *(John 1:1, 14)*, animates alignment with the Divine Nature, that is called fruit: "For the fruit of the Spirit is in all goodness, righteousness, and truth" *(Eph. 5:9)*.

Never Give Up

In first-century Galatia, they could have given up. Arguments among husbands, teachers, leaders, and even some apostles, undoubtedly shook the faith of some Christ-like women in Galatia. Encountering emotional chaos and pain of religious division, they endured the resulting loneliness, isolation, estrangement, and distrust. Ironically, or perhaps because God's ways and thoughts are far above ours, the dark and difficult moments bonded them more closely to Christ. When isolation and disappointment threatened the work of God's Seed in Galatia, women of true faith held fast. As earthly ties unraveled and fleshly identity crumbled, the Spirit's fruit emerged in Galatia. It is the same today.

Conclusion

Did I hear you say that you believe in Jesus? I wrote this to tell you th *Jesus believes in you, too.* He is the incorruptible seed, able to make you whole. He is the living seed, overtaking all the yielded territory of your heart soil. He is the implanted seed, who can masterfully transform yo As Christ grows in you, multiplying like leaven, each aspect of your wil falls down before Him. As a new creation, you are "in Christ" because He was first in you *(Col. 1:27)*. Far beyond the skin-deep color shifting of troublers in Galatia, Christ is creating you anew from the inside out. Obedient-but-free, every woman of faith declares, "It is no longer I who live, but Christ lives in me" *(Gal. 2:20)*. Sowing with unfeigned faith, like Lois and Eunice, "we shall reap if we do not lose heart" *(Gal. 6:9)*.

Many years ago, there was fruit in Galatia.

Thought Questions

1. In your walk of faith, how is skin-deep change different from transformation? Find at least two verses that aid your understanding of this concept.

2. In your understanding, how does copying Jesus exhibit the Spirit's fruit in your life?

3. Although it is a lofty concept, why do you think putting on Christ demands cutting off deeds of flesh? Can you find other New Testament passages that talk about "putting on" or "off"?

4. Define the following terms: feign, unfeigned.

5. In your opinion, what challenges women of faith trying to live "unfeigned"? What are the advantages of wearing the play actor's mask? Practically speaking, what steps could be taken to remove the mask?

6. In your own words, explain the definition of faith. Find at least three passages of Scripture to support your answer.

7. In your opinion, is it feasible in today's world that a woman of faith could impact the world for good by genuine commitment to keeping the home?

8. How could a person manifest her true faith before God and humanity, without works? In the absence of works, what observable evidence proves faith? Find at least two passages that talk about this.

9. What is a success that you have experienced, in which you did things God's way *(even though it was difficult)*, then reaped the beautiful fruit of that choice? What enabled and strengthened you to see it through?

10. Why is it difficult to believe in salvation by faith and salvation by works? Can you think of other examples from the Bible, in which God calls His people to believe in two seemingly contradictory truths?

11. In your own words, explain the Spirit's fruit.

Concept Seeds

To begin preparation for the next phase of your life, consider taking the following challenge:

Choose one facet of the Spirit's fruit. Write an essay about it, addressing how a woman of faith displays that quality in the home, with her husband, with her children, within the local church, and within her community.

Sources

BDAG = Walter Bauer, Frederick William Danker, William F. Arndt, and F. Wilbur Gingrich. *A Greek-English Lexicon of the New Testament and Other Early Christian Literature.* Chicago: University of Chicago Press, 2000.

Lewis, C. S. *Mere Christianity.* New York: HarperOne, 2001.

Gurney, O. "Anatolian religion." *Britannica.com.* https://www.britannica.com/topic/Anatolian-religion.

Guy, Jack. "Who Gets Drunk More Often Than Americans?" *The Mercury News.* May 16, 2019. https://www.mercurynews.com/2019/05/16/who-gets-drunk-more-often-than-americans/.

Pope, Kyle. *How Does the Holy Spirit Work in a Christian?* Athens, AL: Truth Publications, Inc., 2019.

"Synergy." *Merriam-Webster's Collegiate Dictionary.* Springfield, MA: Merriam-Webster, 1996.

CPSIA information can be obtained
at www.ICGtesting.com
Printed in the USA
LVHW072130181021
700807LV00031B/1070